GARDEN BIRDS
OF AMERICA

GARDEN BIRDS OF AMERICA

A Gallery of Garden Birds &
How to Attract Them

by

George H. Harrison

Kit Harrison, Editor

WILLOW CREEK PRESS

Minocqua, Wisconsin

KEY TO RANGE MAPS

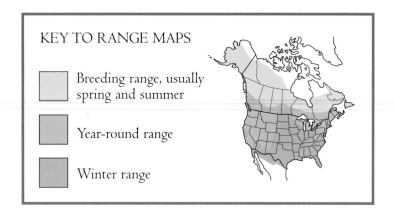

Breeding range, usually spring and summer

Year-round range

Winter range

PHOTOGRAPHY CREDITS
All photographs by the author except: Jerry Pavia, pages 6 and 36; Maslowski Wildlife Productions, pages 23 (bottom), 40, 46 (top), 54, 56, 58, 60, 62 (insert), 66, 74, 92, 98, 102, 106, 108, 110, 122, 132, and 142; and Hal H. Harrison, pages 112, 128, 138 (top), and 152.

2nd printing 1996

Published by WILLOW CREEK PRESS,
P.O. Box 147, Minocqua, WI 54548

For information on other Willow Creek titles,
write or call 1-800-850-WILD.

Design by Patricia Bickner Linder.

Library of Congress Cataloging-in-Publication Data

Harrison, George H.
        Garden birds of America : a gallery of garden birds and how to
    attract them / by George H. Harrison ; Kit Harrison, editor.
            p.   cm.
        ISBN 1-57223-038-X (alk. paper)
        1. Birds--United States.   2. Birds--United States--Pictorial works.
    3. Bird attracting--United States.   4. Gardening to attract birds--
    United States.   I. Harrison, Kit.   II. Title.
        QL682.H365   1996
        598.2973--dc20   95-45966
                                                            CIP

Printed in Canada.

CONTENTS

Introduction, 7

Bird Gardens of America, 11

Garden Birds of America, 38

Backyard Wildlife Habitat Program, 158

INTRODUCTION

magine a half-acre wooded property surrounding a gambrel-roofed house with many windows and skylights, located on a small glacial lake in southeastern Wisconsin, and you have Willowmere. It is a paradise for wild birds, the year around.

During winter, there are at least 12 different kinds of birds on the property at any given moment: chickadees, nuthatches and cardinals at sunflower feeders; various finches eating at niger seed feeders. While woodpeckers tap away at suet feeders on tree trunks, others, such as cedar waxwings, are searching the natural habitat for berries and other fruits, and screech owls are roosting in wood duck houses. On the ground, which is usually covered with snow, sparrows, juncos, mourning doves, and a brilliantly colored cock pheasant peck at bird seeds.

In summer, there are birds in every part of the woods—rose-breasted grosbeaks, cuckoos and wood pewees in the huge oaks, and blue jays in walnuts and ashes, while red-bellied woodpeckers tap at the softer linden trees. In the smaller apple trees, house wrens build nests in hanging birdhouses; in buckthorn, box elder, and highbush cranberry, indigo buntings, yellow warblers and catbirds search for insects and build nests. On the ground among the ferns and pachysandra, the towhees, song sparrows and chipping sparrows forage for seeds and grubs. Hummingbirds zip from the blooming impatiens to the fuchsia to the honeysuckle, sipping nectar as they hover in front of each flower.

Willowmere wasn't always a wild bird paradise. When I purchased it 25 years ago, it was mostly lawn surrounding a tiny seasonal cottage. The transformation began shortly afterward with the planting of a careful selection of food-bearing and cover-producing vegetation to fill all the niches from the ground up. Two recirculating birdbaths were built, birdhouses were situated in various locations to attract the maximum number of tenants, and bird feeders were placed to fill all the feeding niches. We built the Willowmere habitat, and the birds came—nearly 200 different species so far.

Now imagine a honey-colored stone cottage surrounded by a superb flower garden, shade trees, shrubbery, stone walls, and a sheep pasture, and you have Middle Cottage in the English countryside. It, too, is a paradise for wild birds.

For at least three weeks each spring, and again each autumn for the past 10 years, we have happily settled into the 19th Century dwelling with its moss-covered stone-shingled roof for a respite and an indulgence in countryside life.

Our first chore upon arrival each visit is to fill the bird feeder outside the living room window with a mixture of enticing bird seed. Moments later, the first birds appear, followed shortly by small flocks of other British birds that have long ago become very familiar to us.

Like learning to drive on the left side of the highway, it didn't take us long to change our nomenclature for backyard birds at our English residence. In England, the *backyard* is the *garden*, and the birds that are attracted to British gardens are not *backyard birds* but *garden birds*. The *bird feeder* is a *bird table*.

GARDEN BIRDS OF AMERICA

At far left, our English bird garden, complete with a bird table, left, filled with peanuts for tits and a mixture of seeds for green finches and chaffinches.

Next page: An East Hartford, Connecticut, bird garden.

Through the sitting room window, we watch a dozen green finches and a half dozen chaffinches eating bird seeds at the bird table. Every few minutes, a coal tit flits into the table for a sunflower seed, and then retires to the shrubbery to peck it open, then flies back to the table for another.

Beneath the bird table, a brilliantly-colored cock pheasant pecks at the seeds the finches have dropped, while a yellowhammer, a dunnock and a few goldfinches stay out of his way. In the stone wall, a blue tit builds a nest; in the wood shed, a wren does the same. In the pasture, skylarks flutter at breathtaking height, singing their endless chippering song. At night, a little owl calls plaintively from atop the stone wall, while the nightingale sings its lovely melody from the wood.

Thus, we have been very successful in attracting birds to our homes on both sides of the Atlantic. Though the two sites are very different, the ingredients are the same. Both are surrounded by an abundance of natural cover supplemented by birdhouses; both offer a wealth of natural food in the form of berries, nuts, seeds and insects; and both are supplemented by feeder food and water.

The birds in our gardens are a very important part of our daily life on both continents. They give us a great deal of pleasure, fulfillment, and insight into the natural world. They are our link with nature—its beauty, brutality, mystery, and drama.

This book takes something from both worlds as we present the *Garden Birds of America*, 60 of the most interesting and enjoyable birds in North America, and how to attract them to gardens and backyards.

George H. Harrison

BIRD GARDENS
OF AMERICA

ook out your living room window. What do you see?

It's summertime, and the patio garden is lovely. A ruby-throated hummingbird darts into a hanging pot of New Guinea impatiens, drawing a long sip of nectar from a crimson blossom. Then he swoops up to the huge fuchsia plant hanging next to the window. You know that it's a male when the sun illuminates the sequin-like feathers on his ruby throat.

Above the center of the patio, there are six canary-yellow male goldfinches, sporting black caps and wings, eating hulled sunflower seeds from a bird feeder hanging from the basswood tree. Several more goldfinches, mostly males, wait in the spruce tree, not very patiently, for an opening at the feeder.

Farther to the right, a male rose-breasted grosbeak leans into the pool of clear water for a drink. When he straightens up, you can see the large V-shaped red badge on his pure white breast. Next to him, but in water up to his belly, is a male indigo bunting, splashing and dipping enthusiastically, until his deep blue feathers look black from the wetness.

In the red maple, a pair of cardinals wait to bathe and drink. As soon as the pond is available, they'll fly in, and alight side-by-side on the rim of the pool.

A flash of orange and black streaks across the entire length of the patio. It's the male Baltimore oriole, headed for the sugar water feeder that hangs in the box elder.

On the patio bricks, a pair of chipping sparrows is shuffling around, picking up twigs for their nest in the blue spruce along the side of the house. How dapper these two look with their brick-red caps and slate gray breasts. They've been inseparable since early spring.

At the edge of the patio, in the middle of the pot of red geraniums surrounded by purple and white petunias, is a spot of yellow. It's a yellow warbler canvassing the flowers for small caterpillars. He and his mate have a nest of babies in the multiflora rose at the back of your quarter acre.

Beyond the patio, in the entrance to the big birdhouse on the trunk of the tall white ash, is a screech owl—a red phase female. She probably has eggs or young in the house.

Cover for birds year-round includes the discarded family Christmas tree, and a small cedar tree in which a chipping sparrow nests, bottom. Right, Harrison bird garden in Hubertus, Wisconsin.

Every day at about this time she sits in the entrance pretending to be dozing, but watching everything that is going on. She doesn't miss a thing . . . a mouse or a moose, a shrew or a shrike.

Meanwhile, the family of chickadees, complete with their fledgling brood, is about to descend upon the sunflower seed feeder. This is the first visit for the babies, little gray balls of fluff with black caps. Their bedraggled parents try to get them to feed themselves, but no, the youngsters are begging for food . . . and being fed.

All this is going on just outside your favorite window, everyday, throughout the four seasons. If it's not, you are missing something wondrous. But don't despair. Developing a bird garden in your own backyard is easy to do, relatively inexpensive, and will add value to your property. Most importantly, it could add enormously to your quality of life . . . your daily connection with nature in all its beauty, wonder and fulfillment.

Here's how to do it:

THE BASIC INGREDIENTS

All successful bird gardens have three ingredients that are basic requirements for birds . . . indeed, all life on earth: **cover**, **food** and **water**.

COVER

For birds, cover is primarily a diversity of plant life—flowers, shrubs, trees—ranging from the lowest ground cover to the tallest shade trees, and all the plants in between. Cover is also dead trees, fallen logs, rock walls and brush piles.

In the cover, birds find shelter from the weather, hiding places from predators, places to nest, roost, eat, grow up, court, preen, and find food such as insects, fruits, seeds, and nuts.

Though all birds require cover to survive, they do not all require the same kinds of cover. For example, chipping sparrows spend most of their time on or near the ground. They require low-growing trees, shrubs and ground cover, as well as the edges of brushy thickets. They seek small spruces and firs in which they build their cuplike nests lined with hair . . . horse hair if they can find it, but any kind of hair will do.

In contrast, the cover requirement for bluebirds is open grassy fields

where they can find insects and the fruits of blackberries and raspberries. Bluebirds nest adjacent to open fields in cavities of small trees, fence posts, or in birdhouses on fence posts or small trees. They like to have a long approach to their nesting site, and the male sings from nearby trees or utility wires at the edge of the open field.

Tree swallows will also nest in houses, and a bluebird house is the right size for them. However, tree swallows need to be near water where they can gather the kinds of insects that fly over water . . . staple food for them and for their youngsters.

A different kind of cover is required by robins. These yard and garden birds need lawns containing earthworms, but the lawns must be surrounded by trees. Robins build their nests of mud and grass in the crotches of small trees, ornamental evergreens, or on the flat shelves or eaves of houses or sheds.

Cover in the form of birdhouses may be important when there is a lack of the dead trees that cavity-nesting birds require to raise their young. There are 30 some species of birds that will use birdhouses to nest or roost in, with accommodations ranging from a wren house with a one-inch entrance hole, to a huge wood duck house that has a four-inch entrance hole. That's why a bird garden might have a half dozen different kinds of birdhouses in it, most of which could be occupied sometime during the four seasons.

Therefore, a diversity of cover that includes a range of plants from the ground up, plus birdhouses, rock walls and brush piles, will meet the needs of the greatest variety of garden birds on a given property, even in a quarter-acre backyard.

Whorled or yellow loose-strife, top, and hickory, bottom, provide excellent food and cover for birds in a Wisconsin bird garden.

FOOD

Birds glean at least 75 percent of their food from the wild, even when there are bird feeders available to them. Consequently, naturally growing foods are an important element in any successful bird garden. The backyard that has a variety of good cover plants will include many that will also bear food, such as mountain ash that produces orange berries relished by cedar waxwings, robins and cardinals. Serviceberry, an excellent cover plant, yields berries readily consumed by catbirds, bluebirds, and wood thrushes. Hummingbirds require nectar-producing flowers, such as flowering tobacco plants, trumpet creepers, impatiens, and fuchsias.

Food in the bird garden may also mean supplemental food in bird feeders—sugar water for hummingbirds and orioles; hulled sunflower seeds and niger for finches; oil sunflower seeds for cardinals, blue jays, nuthatches, and chickadees; cracked corn for mourning doves; mealworms for bluebirds; and beef suet for woodpeckers. But each of these birds has its own niche in which it feeds. For example, finches prefer to eat from hanging or post feeders at about eye level; cardinals and blue jays from tray feeders where they can get a good perch at table top level; doves, sparrows and juncos on the ground; and woodpeckers on tree trunks where they normally search for insects.

WATER

Birdbaths in many forms will give birds the water they require for drinking and bathing. Birds have to take care of their plumage in order to survive, and that means bathing often to keep their feathers in top flight condition.

If the water moves and splashes, it will be even more appealing to birds, because they will hear the water from some distance and be drawn to it like a magnet. Small pumps can move the water to higher levels, allowing it to flow down to lower levels, making watery noises as it falls.

In addition to providing bathing and drinking water for the feeder birds, the baths will appeal to a broad range of other species that might not otherwise appear in bird gardens. During migration, warblers, vireos, flycatchers, and others en route to or from the tropics may stop for a drink or quick bath. These are bonus birds that will thrill even the casual bird gardener.

Wood ducks nested in this birdhouse located on the edge of a small pond in a Germantown, Wisconsin, bird garden.

THE PLAN

Now that you know the ingredients for a successful bird garden, the next step is to draw a map of your property, showing the location of the house, garage, driveway, lawn, and all existing cover, such as trees, shrubs, hedges, ground cover, rock walls, and so forth. Ask yourself, how much cover, food and water do you already have on your property? What must you plant, grow, build, add, and install to fulfill the needs of the birds you want to entice?

Then, make a list of the items you might need to convert your backyard into a garden bird paradise:

1. Small trees that bear fruit, berries, nuts, or seeds.
2. Small coniferous trees and shrubs in which birds can hide, be protected from weather, and in which they can build nests and raise young.
3. Shrubbery that flowers and bears fruit, berries, nuts, or seeds.
4. Ground cover in which birds can hide, find protection from weather, and in which they can build nests and raise young.
5. Flowers, annuals and perennials, in pots and in beds, that produce brightly colored blossoms, particularly red blossoms to attract hummingbirds.
6. Wild corners of the yard, where the natural vegetation is allowed to grow into mini wildernesses.
7. Brush piles that give ground-inhabiting birds protective cover and places to nest.

First, plot out the existing features of your property, including trees and plants (see example below). Then list the shrubs, trees, other plants, and additional features you wish to add, and map those out on your plan, as in the example at right.

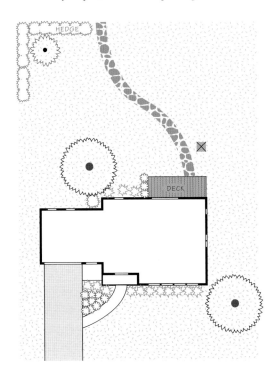

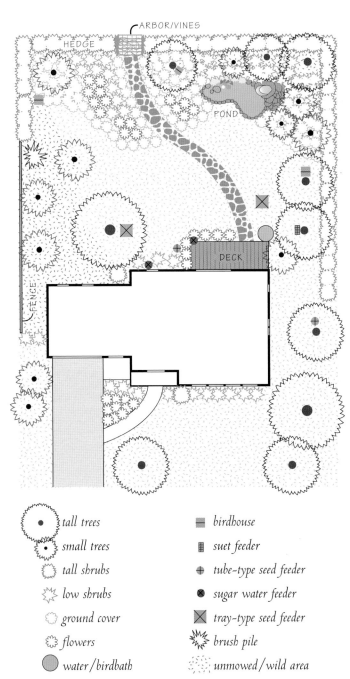

8. Bird feeders — seed, suet and nectar feeders — on the ground, at table-top level, post and hanging, and on tree trunks, covering all the niches that birds fill in a bird garden.

9. Birdbaths, in the form of recirculating ponds and pools, with running water that makes splashing noises and attracts birds from a distance.

tall trees		*birdhouse*	
small trees		*suet feeder*	
tall shrubs		*tube-type seed feeder*	
low shrubs		*sugar water feeder*	
ground cover		*tray-type seed feeder*	
flowers		*brush pile*	
water / birdbath		*unmowed / wild area*	

WHAT TO PLANT

When the list is completed, you might need some advice about what specific plants will grow best in your region and also provide birds with cover and food. Often, the best place to get this kind of help is from a local landscape architecture firm.

Perhaps they would send someone to look at your property and walk it with you. No doubt they will suggest plantings that will be enjoyed for their beauty, while also being attractive to a wide variety of birds throughout the four seasons.

"I'd recommend planting a couple of white pines here, a white ash there, and a hawthorn over there," is the way the dialogue might go. "In that corner, you could plant a bed of elderberry and some autumn olive, and over there some blackberries. Pachysandra would give you great ground cover in that shady spot under those large trees, and a bed of ferns would look lovely along that border," you might be told.

In one short visit, the landscape architect could give you all the advice you need to design a model bird garden in your backyard.

Next, plot the suggested plants on your map . . . white pines here, white ash there, elderberries there, ferns along there, until the map is full of circles and squares, all numbered and keyed to the kinds of plant materials you want to install in the spring.

Mountain ash, top, and sunflower, bottom, are among the best naturally grown bird foods in any bird garden.

Food and Cover Plants for Birds

Northeast

TALL TREES
Coniferous
    White pine
    Hemlock
    Colorado Spruce
Deciduous
    Sugar maple
    White oak
    Red oak
    Beech
    Birch

SMALL TREES
    Flowering dogwood
    Crabapple
    Hawthorn
    Cherry
    Serviceberry
    Red cedar

TALL SHRUBS
    Sumac
    Dogwood
    Highbush cranberry
    Elderberry
    Everbloom honeysuckle
    Winterberry
    Autumn olive
    Wisteria

LOW SHRUBS
    Blackberry
    Blueberry
    Summer sweet
    Red osier dogwood
    Huckleberry
    Snowberry

LOW-GROWING
PLANTS AND FLOWERS
    Panicgrass
    Pachysandra
    Timothy
    Hosta
    Sunflower

Southeast

TALL TREES
Coniferous
    Longleaf pine
    Loblolly pine
    Shortleaf pine
Deciduous
    Ash
    Beech
    Walnut
    Live oak
    Southern red oak
    Black gum
    Pecan
    Hackberry

SMALL TREES
    Holly
    Dogwood
    Serviceberry
    Cherry
    Persimmon
    Red cedar
    Palmetto
    Hawthorn
    Crabapple

TALL SHRUBS
    Sumac
    Dogwood
    Elderberry

LOW SHRUBS
    Blackberry
    Blueberry
    Bayberry
    Spicebush
    Huckleberry

LOW-GROWING
PLANTS AND FLOWERS
    Lespedeya spp.
    Panicgrass
    Sunflower

Northwest

TALL TREES
Coniferous
    Douglas fir
    Ponderosa pine
    Western white pine
    Lodgepole pine
    Colorado Spruce
Deciduous
    Oregon white oak
    California black oak
    Bigleaf maple

SMALL TREES
    Hawthorn
    Serviceberry
    Dogwood

TALL SHRUBS
    Sumac
    Bitterbrush
    Russian olive
    Elderberry
    Buckthorn
    Madrone

LOW SHRUBS
    Blackberry
    Blueberry
    Snowberry
    Oregon grape

LOW-GROWING
PLANTS AND FLOWERS
    Turkeymullein
    Timothy
    Sunflower
    Filaree
    Lupine
    Fiddlenecks
    Tarweed

Southwest

TALL TREES
Coniferous
    Arizona cypress
    Piñon pine
Deciduous
    Live oak
    Pine oak
    Bitter cherry

SMALL TREES
    Serviceberry
    Dogwood
    Mesquite
    Crabapple

TALL SHRUBS
    Mulberry
    Lote bush
    Sumac
    Manzanita
    Madrone

LOW SHRUBS
    Utah juniper
    Blackberry
    Spicebush
    Prickly pear
    Algerita

LOW-GROWING
PLANTS AND FLOWERS
    Turkeymullein
    Sunflower
    Filaree
    Lupine
    Fiddlenecks

BIRD FEEDERS AND FOODS

The next items to plot on the map are bird feeders, the placement of which is critical in two respects: First, they need to be located in or near the kinds of cover into which birds can escape should they be threatened by a neighborhood cat, dog, or winged predator such as a hawk or owl. Otherwise, the birds may not feel safe at the feeders, and may not use them.

The second consideration is to place the feeders close to windows where you can have a good view of them. The reason for providing feeders for wild birds is for the enjoyment of the bird gardener, not for the benefit of the birds, which can survive very well without any help from people. Research on black-capped chickadees, for example, showed that the birds gleaned only 25 percent of their daily food intake from feeders, where available, and the remaining 75 percent from the wild.

With that in mind, place symbols on the map to represent feeders, locating them near cover, as well as close to windows where you can easily see them.

Remember to place several feeders in each of the niches that birds fill when searching for food: on the ground with a wild bird seed mix for mourning doves, dark-eyed juncos, and tree sparrows; some hanging and post feeders filled with sunflower seeds—hulled or black oil—for goldfinches, house finches, chickadees, titmice, and nuthatches; tray feeders at tabletop height with sunflower seeds, mealworms and fruit for cardinals, grosbeaks, blue jays, robins, bluebirds and various kinds of thrushes and thrashers; and on tree trunks with beef suet for woodpeckers, chickadees, blue jays and brown creepers.

During warm months, place feeders containing a four-to-one mixture of sugar water near red flowers outside your favorite windows to bring the hummingbirds and orioles into close range. Orange halves, impaled on nails, will also catch the attention of the orioles, and perhaps others, such as red-bellied woodpeckers.

Purple finches, top, eat sunflower seeds at a Rhinelander, Wisconsin, bird garden.

FREQUENT FEEDERS

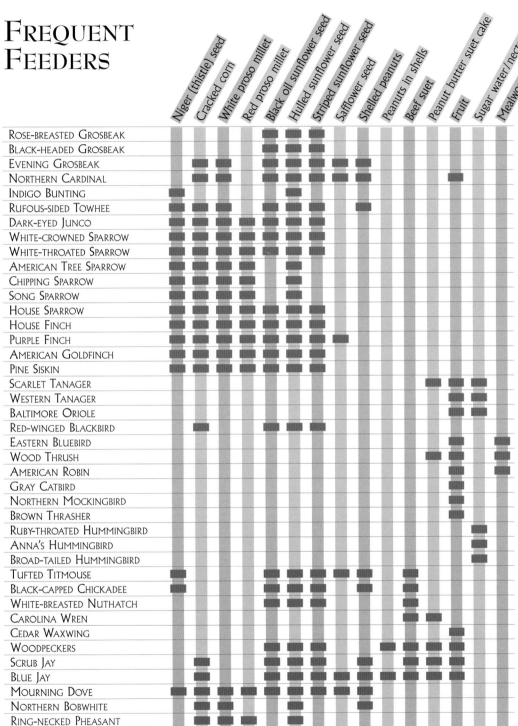

Bird	Niger (thistle) seed	Cracked corn	White proso millet	Red proso millet	Black oil sunflower seed	Hulled sunflower seed	Striped sunflower seed	Safflower seed	Shelled peanuts	Peanuts in shells	Beef suet	Peanut butter suet cake	Fruit	Sugar water/nectar	Mealworms
Rose-breasted Grosbeak					■	■	■								
Black-headed Grosbeak					■	■	■								
Evening Grosbeak		■	■		■	■	■		■						
Northern Cardinal		■	■		■	■	■	■				■			
Indigo Bunting	■					■									
Rufous-sided Towhee	■	■	■		■				■						
Dark-eyed Junco	■	■	■	■	■	■									
White-crowned Sparrow	■	■	■	■		■									
White-throated Sparrow	■	■	■	■		■									
American Tree Sparrow	■	■	■	■		■									
Chipping Sparrow	■	■	■			■									
Song Sparrow	■	■	■			■									
House Sparrow	■	■	■	■		■									
House Finch	■	■	■		■	■									
Purple Finch	■	■	■		■	■		■							
American Goldfinch	■	■	■		■	■									
Pine Siskin	■	■	■		■	■									
Scarlet Tanager											■	■	■		
Western Tanager												■	■		
Baltimore Oriole												■	■		
Red-winged Blackbird		■			■	■	■								
Eastern Bluebird												■			■
Wood Thrush											■	■			■
American Robin												■			■
Gray Catbird													■		
Northern Mockingbird													■		
Brown Thrasher													■		
Ruby-throated Hummingbird														■	
Anna's Hummingbird														■	
Broad-tailed Hummingbird														■	
Tufted Titmouse	■				■	■	■	■	■		■				
Black-capped Chickadee	■				■	■			■						
White-breasted Nuthatch					■	■	■								
Carolina Wren									■		■				
Cedar Waxwing													■		
Woodpeckers					■	■	■			■	■	■	■		
Scrub Jay		■			■	■	■		■	■	■	■			
Blue Jay		■			■	■			■	■	■	■	■		
Mourning Dove	■	■	■	■	■			■							
Northern Bobwhite		■	■		■			■							
Ring-necked Pheasant		■	■	■		■									
Canada Goose		■													
Mallard		■													

BIRDHOUSE SPECIFICATIONS

SPECIES	DIMENSIONS	HOLE	PLACEMENT	COLOR	ADD'L NOTES
EASTERN BLUEBIRD	5" x 5" x 8"h.	1-1/2" centered 6" above floor	5-10' high in the open, sunny	light earth tones	likes open areas esp. facing a field
TREE SWALLOW	5" x 5" x 6"h.	1-1/2" centered 4" above floor	5-8' high in the open 50-100% sun	light earth tones; gray	within 2 miles of pond or lake
PURPLE MARTIN	multiple apartments 6" x 6" x 6" ea.	2-1/2" hole 2-1/4" above floor	15-20' high in the open	white	open yard without tall trees; near water
TUFTED TITMOUSE	4" x 4" x 8"h.	1-1/4"	4-10' high	light earth tones	prefers in or near wooded area
CHICKADEE	4" x 4" x 8"h. or 5" x 5" base	1-1/8" centered 6" above floor	4-8' high	light earth tones	small tree thicket
NUTHATCH	4" x 4" x 10"h.	1-1/4" centered 7-1/2" above floor	12-25' high on tree trunk	bark covered; natural	
HOUSE WREN	4" x 4" x 8"h. or 4" x 6" base	1" centered 6" above floor	5-10' high on post or hung in tree	white; light earth tones	
NORTHERN FLICKER	7" x 7" x 18"h.	2-1/2" centered 14" above floor	8-20' high	light earth tones	put 4" sawdust inside for nesting
DOWNY WOODPECKER	4" x 4" x 10"h.	1-1/4" centered 7-1/2" above floor	12-25' high on tree trunk	simulate natural cavity	prefers own excavation provide sawdust
RED-HEADED WOODPECKER	6" x 6" x 15"h.	2" centered 6-8" above floor	8-20' high post or tree trunk	simulate natural cavity	needs sawdust for nesting
WOOD DUCK	10" x 10" x 24"h.	4" x 3" elliptical 20" above floor	post 2-5' high over water or on tree 12-40' high facing water	light earth tones; natural	needs 3-4" sawdust or shavings for nesting
AMERICAN KESTREL	10" x 10" x 24"h.	4" x 3" elliptical 20" above floor	12-40' high on post or tree	light earth tones; natural	needs open approach on edge of woodlot or in isolated tree
SCREECH OWL	10" x 10" x 24"h.	4" x 3" elliptical 20" above floor	post 2-5' high over water or on tree 12-40' high	light earth tones; natural	prefers open woods or edge of woodlot
NESTING PLATFORMS					
AMERICAN ROBIN BARN SWALLOW PHOEBE	6" x 6" x 8"h. needs roof for rain protection	none	on side of building or arbor or in tree	lt. earth tones; wood	use is irregular prefers open country prefers water nearby

Note: With the exception of wrens, birds do not tolerate swaying birdhouses. Birdhouses should be firmly anchored to a post, a tree, or the side of a building.

BIRDHOUSES

Next, plot where to place birdhouses on the property. Though more than 30 kinds of birds will use birdhouses, only about a half dozen are garden birds.

If your property is located along a body of water, lake, pond or stream, consider placing wood duck houses on the shoreline, either on the trunks of trees, or on posts. Be sure that the 10" x 10" x 24"-high house is facing your favorite window, because when it becomes occupied, you'll want to be able to watch the activity. And don't be surprised if a screech owl takes over the house as a roosting box during winter, and perhaps even in spring to produce its own family. An American kestrel may also like the wood duck house, if it is in or near an open field.

Wren houses can be hung from fruit trees, or placed on posts at eye level around the yard, in or near cover. It would not be out of line to place at least three wren houses in the garden area, as the male will fill them all with sticks, and the female will then choose one for the family. Wren houses can be a variety of sizes and shapes, but they need to have a small entrance hole of not more than 1-1/8".

If a house has an entrances hole of 1-1/4" to 1-1/2", it may become the nesting site for a family of chickadees, or if the house is placed on the edge of an open field or garden, bluebirds or tree swallows will investigate it and possibly move in.

Middle size houses, 4" x 4" x 18"-high, will appeal to woodpeckers. Northern flickers or red-bellied woodpeckers are the most likely residents, but there is also the possibility of a red-headed woodpecker pair taking a fancy to a house and claiming it for their own.

All houses should be cleaned at least once a year. The smaller houses can be stored during winter, but the larger houses can be left as possible winter roosting sites for any number of interesting birds.

Tree swallow, top, and eastern phoebe, bottom, often nest in garden birdhouses and shelters in many regions of America.

BIRDBATHS

Don't forget to place one or two birdbaths around the garden. They can be either the traditional bowl on a pedestal, which requires fresh water daily, or a more elaborate set of pools at various levels in which the water is moved with an electric pump. The advantage to the moving water is that its pleasant splashing sound will attract many more birds.

Regardless of the kind of birdbath you install, be sure that it, too, is located within good viewing distance of the best window.

GETTING IT DONE

Once the plan is complete, the work can follow, and the results will be immediately realized. Every bird gardener has different capabilities in time and financial means, and each has to determine the extent of the bird garden project. But even the smallest effort with the least investment will produce worthwhile results, and the rewards will be great. The following pages contain examples of the kinds of experiences that can be expected as a result of establishing and maintaining even a modest bird garden.

A gray catbird, top, makes the most of a recirculating pool in the Harrison bird garden, far left.

HUME, VIRGINIA

The hen wood duck sat in the entrance of the birdhouse some 30 feet above the ground in an ash tree. Yet something was very different about her appearance. It was 6:30 a.m. She had never before just sat in the entrance. She had always exited and entered the house over the past month or so at break-neck speed, without any hesitation. On this morning, something was very different; something was about to happen.

She looked this way and that way, checking to see if there was any danger above her or below her. As she turned her long graceful neck, it appeared that she was being bumped from behind . . . nearly pushing her out of the house. Was there something inside trying to get out?

Rose hips, containing the seeds of roses, are superb food for birds in many bird gardens. At right, a bird garden in Hume, Virginia.

After what seemed to be endless observing of her surroundings, she dropped out of the house and to the ground. Alighting at the base of the tree, she uttered a quiet *quack*.

Instantly, a little downy yellow duckling appeared in the house entrance, hesitated for a split second, and then pushed off into midair, furiously flapping its stubby wings as it dropped the 30 feet to the ground, bounced around like a yellow tennis ball, and then came upright next to the hen.

Another duckling was in the entrance . . . then two more . . . each pushing off and parachuting to the ground. Three more at a time . . . two more. The count was eight, ten, twelve, then sixteen, all dropping to the ground and swirling around the mother duck in a flow of down-covered energy.

After number sixteen, there were no more. The hen called, but nothing appeared at the entrance. The evacuation was complete.

Apparently satisfied, she led the brood across the grassy terrace to the lake shore and eased herself into the water, followed very closely by the yellow stream of peeping ducklings . . . and they all disappeared into the protection of aquatic vegetation.

The brood of wood ducks would spend the next two months growing up in the marshy lake, learning the ways of the wild, and preparing for their long flight south for winter. There they would find mates, and in the following spring each young hen would lead her chosen mate back to the very same lake on which she was raised. If the house in which she was hatched was unoccupied, she would probably settle into it to produce the next generation of woodies.

SOUTHWEST HARBOR, MAINE

The black-capped chickadees had spent the winter at the feeders, eating sunflower seeds and an occasional snack of beef suet where the woodpeckers ate.

Black-capped chickadees nest in tree cavities, but may be enticed to use a birdhouse located in a small tree thicket.

But they hung around as the spring weather changed the bird garden from a collection of drab sleeping plants to a lively circus of brilliant flowers.

Then one day in early June, the chickadees were seen carrying nesting material into a small hole in a dead silver birch sapling. The woodpeckers must have made the hole, and the chickadees decided to move in. A few days later, the first of six white eggs was laid, followed by one a day for five more days.

The female began the long incubation period while the male carried insect morsels to her during her incarceration in the cavity. But when the eggs hatched, both parents fed the increasingly hungry brood. About every ten to fifteen minutes, both adults would fly to the entrance of the nesting cavity with a caterpillar or small flying insect, and disappear into the sapling.

When the youngsters fledged the nest, it seemed that the bird garden was full of chickadees, all fluttering their wings, following their parents, begging for food. The little balls of black and white cotton followed their parents to the sunflower feeders, being fed at first. Soon they were selecting their own seed, flying to a nearby branch, placing the seed between their black feet and hammering the morsel with their tiny, sharp, black bills until the meat broke into edible pieces. What a show!

HELENA, MONTANA

The invasion was on. Wave after wave of finches and grosbeaks from the boreal forests of Canada and Alaska swept into the bird gardens where sunflower seed, niger and millet were offered in a variety of bird feeders.

These hordes of hungry birds had been forced out of their traditional northern ranges in search of food. Their expanded numbers, combined with a failure of the boreal trees to produce a good crop of seeds, caused this massive southern and eastern movement of desperate birds in search of food.

Fluttering around the hanging tube feeders filled with niger seeds, pine siskins and redpolls fought each other for a perch from which they could extract the tiny black seeds.

On a large tray feeder, the one piled high with black oil sunflower seeds, more commotion could be seen and heard as the dark yellow male evening grosbeaks and their silvery female counterparts each defended its own square inch of feeding space.

On the ground beneath the hanging and post feeders, dark-eyed juncos, American tree sparrows and mourning doves picked up the discards that were dropped or rejected by the bedlam of birds above.

The number of birds that visit garden feeders during winters like this is limited only by the amount of food that is available. At some, bushels of seeds are consumed in a single day. But the sight and sounds of a horde of northern invaders is well worth the effort to keep them contented.

HUBERTUS, WISCONSIN

It was late — almost too late for cardinals to be nesting, but there they were, busy building a flimsy stick nest in the shrubbery just outside the garage window. By mid-August, most cardinals have already fledged at least one brood, and some two. Apparently this couple had experienced the destruction of earlier nests, perhaps by chipmunks, raccoons, blue jays or crows.

Three brown-spotted eggs were dutifully incubated by the female cardinal for 12 days, during which time the brilliant red male carried food to her on the nest. As soon as the eggs hatched, both parents became busy stuffing food into little red mouths. They brought green caterpillars, dragonflies and blackberries, all to be deposited into the widest, most demanding mouth.

Normally, cardinal hatchlings remain in the nest for about 12 days, but this brood, with its very late start, seemed to be growing quicker than others, and they were restless and already preening a mantle of brown feathers well before the end of the 12-day period. Suddenly, they were up and out, scattering into the garden shrubbery, *chirping* loudly so their

Among the most exciting winter visitors to bird gardens throughout America are evening grosbeaks.

parents could find them and feed them for a few more days until they could capture and consume their own food.

But the best part of the cardinal show was the day the youngsters followed a parent to the tray feeder, where the old bird showed them the unhulled sunflower seeds, and how to eat them. In a few more days, the black-billed youngsters were at the feeder on their own, eating with great skill, as if they knew how to do it all along.

WATERSONVILLE, PENNSYLVANIA

This spring was different than other springs for the house wrens. Each year they had built a stick nest in every available birdhouse on the property. But this year, a new house was being constructed on the property, and there were piles of soil, equipment and vehicles everywhere. Workmen were all over the grounds, all day long, and the noise of machinery was deafening.

Yet, the male house wren, master of all he surveyed, was not to be deterred. He arrived from the South on schedule, set up his territory, and began to sing his non-stop, bubbling, chattering, repetitive burst of melody. He also built dummy nests in all the available birdhouses, and one in the grill of a dump truck that was parked in the driveway.

When a female arrived on the scene a week later, she inspected all of his dummy nest work in the various birdhouses around the property. But she took a fancy to the nest in the grill of the truck. That, she decided, was the best location of all. She then removed all of his sticks, and built a proper wren nest that suited her. By then, the workers had to promise not to move the truck while the wrens were in residence. Into the nest the female laid eight tiny, brown-spotted eggs, and began her 13 days of incubation, by herself, day and night.

Baby northern cardinal, top, and baby house wren, bottom, are learning to fly in a Wisconsin bird garden. At left, a bird garden in Hubertus, Wisconsin.

Meanwhile, the male sang on and on, from every twig and branch of his territory, proclaiming that this was his, and all other wrens should stay away. All others, that is, except any unattached females that happened along. These he courted enthusiastically, until one settled into another of his prefab nesting sites.

Much to the workmen's chagrin, the dump truck was destined to remain stationary on the driveway for nearly a month while the little female house wren incubated eggs, then fed and raised the babies. Finally, the offspring fledged, all eight leaving the truck's grill in a matter of a few seconds. The dump truck was then allowed to be moved.

Despite the construction of a new house, the bird garden surrounding it produced three broods of house wrens totaling more than 20 youngsters during the summer of construction.

DES MOINES, IOWA

The top tier of the bird pond is only three feet in diameter, but it is a very busy place during hot summer days.

By the time baby robins are out of the nest and old enough to feed themselves, they have discovered that the bird pond is a great place to meet, greet, and squabble with other teenagers; but most of all, it's a great place to get wet.

A northern cardinal is just one of dozens of birds that frequent the recirculating pools at the Harrison bird garden. At right, a bird garden in Des Plaines, Illinois.

One day, there were nine baby robins on and in the top pool. All were at about the same stage of development ... spotted brick-red breasts, charcoal-gray backs ... and inexperienced about the ways of the wild.

Two or three at a time would wade in, dip their heads into the water and splash as much as they could. Water sprayed everywhere, in and out of the pond and all over the patio. It was like the 4th of July at the local park swimming pool.

The young robins were also establishing a pecking order, even while bathing. Those that were to be dominant moved into the water and chased their subordinates out of the pool ... sort of like playing "king of the bath."

Other birds—indigo buntings, Baltimore orioles, cardinals and goldfinches—all attempted to get into the water, but there were too many bathers there already. They would come back later.

A black-capped chickadee, top, finds nourishment in sunflower seeds early on a northern winter morning, top. A ruby-throated hummingbird sips sugar water from a feeder at a bird garden in Spruce Creek, Pennsylvania.

MADISON, WISCONSIN

It was one of the coldest winters on record. The black-capped chickadees and white-breasted nuthatches stuck together in roving bands of gypsy birds, searching for spider eggs, wood borers, weed seeds, berries, and the sunflower seeds offered in bird gardens.

When night came, the little birds got out of the weather as best they could, bundling into tree cavities and birdhouses and into clumps of dead leaves. Here they placed their bills under a wing, fluffed up their feathers to trap their body heat, and fell asleep. During sleep, they slowed their metabolism, reduced the number of heartbeats, and lowered their blood pressure and body temperatures, all to conserve energy through the long, dark, and very cold night.

Upon awakening, the chickadees were low on body fat, and had to find food quickly or perish in the extreme cold. Rejoining the band of fellow scavengers, they flitted from one nook and cranny to another, where they found the kind of high protein food they needed. At bird gardens, the sunflower seed they gleaned from feeders also gave them the boost they needed to restock their body fats. The chickadees would survive another day.

ROCKPORT, TEXAS

Most ruby-throated hummingbirds cross the Gulf of Mexico in early September en route to their wintering grounds in Central and South America. During that period, ruby-throats by the thousands often congregate on the Gulf Coast of Texas waiting for the right weather conditions before launching off on their 500-mile long flight across open water. While they wait, they continue to fuel up on nectar, insects and sugar water from local feeders.

Bird gardeners in the Rockport area cater to the tiny travelers by planting plenty of nectar-rich, tubular flowers in their gardens, and by hanging out an abundance of hummingbird feeders containing sugar water.

This annual phenomenon has become so spectacular that the Rockport-Fulton Chamber of Commerce holds a Hummer/Bird Celebration at the Junior High School on the second weekend in September. Bird watchers are invited to attend the affair, which includes tours of some 40 bird gardens in the area where hummingbirds are being fed. For more information, call 1-800-242-0071.

BLACKWELL, OKLAHOMA

Stubby was first noticed in late winter eating cracked corn at the tray feeder with a half dozen other mourning doves. She appeared to be healthy except that one of her red feet was missing. She had only a stub of a leg on that side.

A few weeks later, Stubby was back at the feeder, but this time she was the focus of attention of a handsome male mourning dove sporting iridescent neck feathers that he puffed up at the peak of his courtship display for her. Stubby seemed to be paying no attention. Yet the courting and cooing by the male continued for several more days as the spring weather brightened and temperatures rose.

The next time Stubby was seen, she was carrying a twig in her bill to the blue spruce tree in the corner of the yard where she piled it on top of several other sticks in what appeared to be the start of a nesting platform.

Fuchsia blossoms contain nectar relished by hummingbirds and orioles in bird gardens across America.

In spite of the fact that she was working at a disadvantage with only one foot, Stubby finished her nest in a few more days, laid two pure white eggs in it, and began the two week incubation. The activity at the nest increased when the eggs hatched and both parents fed the little ones.

When Stubby's youngsters were old enough to fly, they plopped onto the same tray feeder where their parents had courted a month or so earlier, and camped out on it for hours. The young doves had already learned the fine art of loafing.

The show that Stubby and her mate put on continued through two more nestings, and soon the garden was well populated with Stubby's offspring.

CARLSBAD, NEW MEXICO

Greater roadrunners were common birds in the garden, but strangely, only adults were seen, never youngsters.

Then one spring, a roadrunner was spotted carrying twigs into a shrub at the edge of the garden. The nest was about six feet above the ground, and very well hidden. Later, the bird was seen carrying a snake skin into the nest.

Then, after nearly three weeks had passed with no visible activity at the nest, the parent birds were busy again carrying food to it. To get to the nest, the parent birds would climb the nearby oak, and after watching for danger for a few minutes, they would jump across to the shrub and disappear into the nest.

The mystery of why there were never any baby roadrunners around was solved when the youngsters finally emerged full-sized from the nest, looking exactly like their parents.

At left, a bird garden in California. The greater roadrunner, above, is a quiet but exciting visitor to bird gardens in the Southwest.

PORTLAND, OREGON

A poncho was draped over a wooden stick man sitting in a chair on the deck overlooking the bird garden. Sunflower seeds filled the two plastic cups held in the gloved hands of the stick man. To these cups, chickadees, nuthatches and pine siskins flew regularly, where they perched on the rims and ate the seeds.

Every few days, the creators of this stick man would replace him with themselves. Draped under the poncho, they held the cups of seeds in their gloved hands and waited for the birds to come. The birds came almost immediately every time.

This deception was so successful and so much fun, that neighborhood children began to visit the bird gardeners so that they could take a turn sitting under the poncho feeding the birds. Imagine the excitement of having a sprightly chickadee only a few inches away.

ROSE-BREASTED GROSBEAK

A resplendent male rose-breasted grosbeak, surrounded by lush green leaves, perches on an oak branch high above the garden, its ruby-red breast pushed out, black head raised skyward, projecting a robinlike carol that fills the air with music.

Suddenly, the bird stops singing, and turns its head skyward to watch a red-tailed hawk soaring. It listens to the raptor's scream, and then chips an alarm as it flies from the branch, creating a twirling illusion caused by the rapid movement of its black wings with large white spots. The delicate pink underlinings of the bird's wings flash as it flies overhead.

The rose-breasted grosbeak male is a symphony of color and song that lasts throughout the summer. In sharp contrast, the female rose-breasted grosbeak is dressed in a drab, brown-streaked, sparrowlike plumage, so different from her mate that many people do not connect the two as a pair.

The two sexes don't even arrive in the North together from their wintering grounds in Mexico, Central and South America. The males set up territories first, and permeate the woodland with song and display by the time the females land some 10 days later. Early on, it is not unusual to see four or five males and three or four females all eating sunflower seeds together at a garden tray feeder. But as spring progresses, and pairs bond, fewer rosebreasts visit feeders and bathing pools.

The grosbeak pair share nesting duties, including incubation of eggs and feeding of young, while both continue to sing their lovely carol throughout. Rose-breasted youngsters resemble their mother, except that young males show rose coloring under their wings. By the time the fledglings join their parents at feeders, the oldsters are showing signs of changing their breeding plumages to plainer winter garbs. And then one day in late summer, the rose-breasteds are gone for another year.

ATTRACTED TO:
tall trees, shrubbery,
feeders, water, insects

BLACK-HEADED GROSBEAK

The first thing the campers did upon arrival at a campground in southeastern Arizona was to place a cupful of sunflower seeds on the nearest big rock, and then wait to see who came to dinner.

A few minutes later, a male black-headed grosbeak fluttered to the rock, his rich orange and black plumage with white wing bars sparkling in the late afternoon sunlight. Then a female joined him, with her pattern of warm brown and white stripes. Using their heavy conical bills, they efficiently cracked the sunflower seeds.

These entirely western grosbeaks are typically tame and slow-moving around campgrounds, parks and backyard gardens. The male's lovely robinlike song, with trills and short phrases, is a delight to hear.

In spring, the males return from Mexico to their western United States and Canadian breeding grounds ahead of the females, stake out territories in orchards, woodlands and suburban backyards, and begin singing. A few days later, when the females arrive, the males' singing intensifies, sometimes while they hover above the females.

All the fuss eventually gets the females interested in building bulky nests, some 4 to 12 feet above the ground in the fork of a tree. The 3 to 4 eggs are incubated by both parents, and both may sing as they take their turn on the nest. They also share in feeding caterpillars and other insects and berries to the young until they are old enough to feed themselves.

These lovely birds of summer will readily accept sunflower seeds in any form offered in tray feeders, and will visit garden birdbaths to drink and bathe throughout the warm summer months.

ATTRACTED TO:
tall trees, shrubbery,
feeders, water, insects

EVENING GROSBEAK

s the first light of a cold February day filters from a dark gray sky, a cacophony of *chip* and *chirp, clee-ip* is heard in the birch trees above. The volume suddenly increases as a flock of two dozen evening grosbeaks falls out of the trees and glides to the back deck of a house where trays of sunflower seeds await their visit.

These dramatic birds of winter—northern coniferous forest inhabitants—irrupt into northern and middle America every few years when food in their forest habitat is scarce. It is during these special winters that people who have the time and resources to offer an endless supply of sunflower seeds are rewarded with an evening grosbeak show of a lifetime.

Though they are very gregarious birds, the grosbeaks constantly fight at feeders, vying for position, chasing each other away, and chattering all the while. The result is bedlam, but what fun to watch as the gold and black males and the silvery-yellow females mix at the feeding trays. Their large greenish-white bills are built for cracking tree seeds, and they can easily crack open seeds of sunflowers. In addition to the food, evening grosbeaks will drink and even bathe in heated water, should it be made available.

In summer, these birds remain in flocks, even while courting and nesting high in northern conifers. The female builds a loose nest of mosses and lichens, into which she lays three to four eggs, raising the young on a diet of insects.

Though they may be infrequent visitors to most gardens in winter, when the evening grosbeaks do arrive, it is cause for celebration, for they are perhaps the most colorful and exciting feeder birds of all.

ATTRACTED TO:
tall trees, shrubbery, feeders, water

Northern Cardinal

 n richness of plumage, elegance of motion, and strength of song, [the cardinal] surpasses all its kindred in the United States," wrote John James Audubon. No other garden bird in America is a more welcomed visitor than the northern cardinal.

Like the flowers of the red impatiens, the male cardinal blooms throughout the summer, whistling *what-cheer, what-cheer, birdie, birdie, birdie,* from the first bright days of February to the last humid days of August. Here is a garden bird for all seasons.

Yet, as attractive as this flying monk in red robes is, his mate's subtle beauty is an equally stunning arrangement of olive-buff, accessorized with red wings, crest and bill. She can even match his song, albeit with a somewhat softer rendition.

When spring is in the air, the male cardinal's fancy turns to courting his mate with not-too-subtle offerings of sunflower seeds, passed from bill to bill. This results in the two finding a suitable nesting site in dense garden shrubbery, where they build a flimsy nest of twigs, vines and rootlets. While the female incubates the three or four eggs, the male makes frequent trips to the nest with tidbits of her favorite foods. Both parents feed the nestlings caterpillars and other insects until they are old enough to feed themselves.

Baby cardinals are delightful to watch at feeders. They're already quite adept at cracking sunflower seeds, a favorite food, with their large, sharp bills. Though their bills are still black, their fawn-brown juvenile plumage already reveals whether they are males or females by the amount of red that shows through.

Cardinals are generally stay-at-home birds that spend the four seasons in the same gardens, and remain mated throughout the year.

Attracted to:
*small trees, shrubbery,
feeders, water, insects*

INDIGO BUNTING

ot summer afternoons are made lovely by the lazy *sweet, sweet; zee, zee; seer, seer; sip, sip* rhythm of the indigo bunting's song from a nearby woodland clearing. To catch a glimpse of this unbelievable deep blue bird eclipsed in lush green foliage begs the question: could such a colorful bird exist, or is it a figment of the imagination?

Adding to the fairy tale is the notion that male indigo buntings may not be blue at all. When wet, or when the rays of the sun do not hit them right, the bunting's blue appears brown or black. But only after the breeding season is over do male indigo buntings actually change their striking blue summer garbs for a mostly earthy-brown plumage, retaining only a hint of blue in their wings and tails.

Females are never blue. They are always buffy sparrowlike birds with only a very faint wash of blue in their wing feathers. This coloration makes them nearly invisible while sitting on nests in shrubbery.

Indigo buntings add color, music and animation to many garden scenes where they are attracted to food and water. Like other finches, they are primarily seed eaters, and may accept offerings of niger and sunflower seeds from garden feeders. They seem to enjoy the frequent splash in the garden pool, where their blue feathers quickly turn black when wet.

Regrettably, their stay in the North is not long enough. Indigo buntings are long-distance migrators, flying all the way to Mexico, the West Indies, and to Central and South America for the winter, and they are gone from the North by the end of August.

ATTRACTED TO:
small trees, shrubbery, vines, feeders, water, insects

RUFOUS-SIDED TOWHEE

cratch, scuffle, rattle, scuffle, rattle, scratch. What's all that noise in the underbrush? It sounds like a squirrel scuffling in the dead leaves. There it is: it's a bird. Is it a robin? No ... too much black. *Towwheee.* Oh, its a rufous-sided towhee.

See how it scratches in the leaves, shuffling both feet to the rear at the same time. How does it keep from falling on its face? Clever bird, the towhee.

It identifies itself with its call, as do the chickadee, phoebe, bobwhite, and killdeer. But the male towhee also sings a most pleasant *drink-your-teeeee* song from the tallest shrub in his territory, announcing to all who hear that spring has arrived and it's time to get to the business of building a nest and raising young. Perhaps that's why towhees seem to be busy, busy, busy.

Because the towhee's rufous flanks resemble the brick-red breast of the American robin, it has been nicknamed "ground robin." Yet, the male's black back and the female's brown back and their white bellies distinguish them from the robin when observed up close. Towhees also flash white on their wings and outer tail feathers when they fly.

Rufous-sided towhees often frequent gardens where there are wild and brushy corners in which they can scratch in the leaves in search of the insects, seeds and fruits their diets demand. These ground-loving thicket birds may select that same part of the garden in which to build their bulky nest of leaves, twigs, grasses and weed stalks, all gathered within a radius of 60 feet.

In the North, towhees usually produce two broods of about three to five young each; in the South, the summer may be long enough to allow a third brood.

ATTRACTED TO:
shrubbery, ground cover, vines, brush piles, feeders, water, insects

Dark-eyed Junco

No wonder they are called "snowbirds." Like magic, dark-eyed juncos appear at garden bird feeders with the first snowflakes of the winter, and they remain faithful winter residents until the last snowflake falls in early spring. When you see *one*, you see a small flock of juncos, as they are gregarious birds.

In winter, these dapper slate-gray birds with white bellies and white outer tail feathers eat the seeds, buds and sprouts that they find on the ground. To uncover the food, they perform a jaunty foraging dance by shuffling backwards with both feet. The more snow on the ground, the more shuffling they must do. It is amusing to watch a flock of juncos all dancing the junco shuffle at once.

As spring nears, the male dark-eyed juncos begin to sing their lovely musical song, a short, fast trill. When they are alarmed, they sound off with a metallic *chink* note.

For most gardeners, winter is the time for seeing dark-eyed juncos, because they disappear as soon as warm weather invades. The birds head for northern or high altitude coniferous forests where they build mossy nests under secluded banks or fallen logs, and raise four to five young.

In the West, dark-eyed juncos have slightly different appearances, depending on the region. Some in the Northwest have all-black hoods on brown backs and white bellies; in the Southwest, they have gray heads with rusty backs. The white outer tail feathers are consistent among all juncos.

They all appear to be fond of millet, cracked corn or hulled sunflower seeds, and if it is placed in tray feeders, on or near the ground, the juncos will come, and they will enhance the winter garden scene as long as the snow flies.

Attracted to:
*shrubbery, ground cover,
vines, brush piles, feeders*

WHITE-CROWNED SPARROW

**A**s the car came to a stop in the parking lot at Point Lobos State Reserve on the 17-Mile-Drive in California, a pair of white-crowned sparrows landed on the front bumper and began to pick off the insects that had been smashed on the car's grill. These two had learned through experience that each new car that arrived in the parking lot brought with it a fresh supply of insects, free for the picking.

This pair was also quite tame, and made friends as soon as the sandwiches and cookies appeared. As they ate crumbs from the hand it was a delight to see their high, puffy, white and black striped crowns, pale throats, gray breasts and brown streaked backs. Their sharp, pink bills picked up the food, even while calling a smart *seet* note. When the food had been put away, and all the insects plucked from the car's grill, the aristocratic-looking male mounted the tallest weed stock in the parking lot and sang a sad whistle, followed by a jumbled trill.

Though this pair was nesting nearby—a part of the West Coast breeding population—many white-crowned sparrows migrate to the far North to build their nests on or near the ground. In a cup of fine twigs, grasses, feathers and hair, the female incubates 4 to 5 eggs for about 12 days. In another 10 days, the young are ready to leave the nest.

It is during migrations to and from the nesting grounds that most white-crowned sparrows visit gardens in small flocks, as far south as the Gulf Coast. They are interested in flower and weed seeds or any bird seeds they can find on or under feeders. Though the males may entertain with their plaintive whistle songs, just watching them is a pleasure.

ATTRACTED TO:
shrubbery, ground cover,
vines, brush piles, feeders

WHITE-THROATED SPARROW

ts song is very delicate and plaintive—a thin, wavering, tremulous whistle, which disappoints one, however, as it ends when it seems only to have begun. If the bird could give us the finished strain of which this seems only the prelude, it would stand first among feathered songsters," claimed John Burroughs in *Wake-Robin.*

Yet, for many gardeners, the white-throated sparrow's simple *Old Sam Peabody, Peabody, Peabody* is one of the loveliest of all bird songs and is eagerly anticipated each year from late winter into spring. Though there are some slight regional differences, there seems to be a great deal of disagreement about what the white-throated sparrow is actually singing. In Canada, for example, gardeners are positive that the whitethroats are singing, *Oh, sweet Canada, Canada, Canada.*

Named for the distinctive white throat patch, both male and female also have white and black striped crowns, yellow patches in front of their eyes, streaked brown backs and gray breasts. They may be confused with white-crowned sparrows that migrate through the same gardens during spring and fall, but the whitecrowns pass through about two weeks earlier, and have no white throats. Both spend a great deal of their lives on the ground in search of seeds from flowers, weeds and bird feeders. Like whitecrowns, whitethroats migrate in small flocks of their own kind, often calling a forceful *chink* as they scratch around in dead leaves beneath the undergrowth.

Though white-throated sparrows winter across the deep South, most gardeners see them only when the birds are en route to or from their breeding grounds in the North. In the autumn, sharp-eyed gardeners may spot the heavily-striped youngsters, with pale white throats and crowns, heading south for the winter.

ATTRACTED TO:
shrubbery, ground cover, vines, brush piles, feeders

AMERICAN TREE SPARROW

hen the early colonists arrived in America, they found new world birds that reminded them of those they had known in Europe. That is why they named some of them for the Old World look-alikes. One such bird is the American tree sparrow, that was vaguely reminiscent of the European tree sparrow, but in appearance only. In fact, the American tree sparrow spends most of its time on the ground, not in trees; it eats on the ground and it nests on or near the ground. Though the colonists may have been well-intentioned, their name for the American tree sparrow is a misnomer.

Regardless, American tree sparrows are delightful little sprites that spend their winters in the United States, often at garden bird feeders, and their summers in the treeless tundra of the Arctic where they raise one brood of five or six young per pair.

When you see one tree sparrow in the garden, you will see several, as they winter in wandering bands, whispering tinkling calls reminiscent of sleigh bells as they scour the snow-covered landscape for weed seeds, or for bird seeds beneath hanging feeders. The colder the winter, the more tree sparrows that invade from the North.

On very cold winter nights, tree sparrows may seek shelter off the ground for roosting. Two dried tree sparrow bodies were found beneath the nest of a house wren when a New Hampshire gardener cleaned the birdhouse in late summer after the wrens had vacated it. Apparently, the two tree sparrows had frozen to death the previous winter as they sought to find protection from the bitter cold.

In April, just before heading to their breeding grounds in the far North, males tune up their cheerful, trilling song in a kind of farewell performance in gardens across America.

ATTRACTED TO:
shrubbery, ground cover,
vines, brush piles, feeders

CHIPPING SPARROW

amed for its song, a chipping insectlike trill, the chipping sparrow is among the tamest of all garden birds in America. Any time there is work to be done in the garden, the chipping sparrows seem to be around as inconspicuous but friendly companions.

The "chippy" is simply a natty little ground sparrow with a brick-red cap. The only other garden birds with similar red caps are the American tree sparrow, a winter bird with a black dot in the middle of its breast, and the field sparrow, with a pink bill. Yet, the chipping sparrow alone seems to be attracted to people, and is at home in gardens throughout the summer months, searching for seeds and insects on the ground.

Male chippies arrive in the North in April, about the time that the look-alike tree sparrows are leaving for their breeding grounds much farther north. The male chippies set up small territories in yards and gardens and begin their trilling songs. When the females arrive a week or so later, pairs are formed that appear inseparable for the rest of the season.

A small evergreen in the yard near the garden is the site of most chipping sparrow nests. The pair will build a little cup nest of fine grasses and weed stalks and line it with some kind of hair, sometimes human hair. The 4 dark-blotched, bluish green eggs are incubated by the female for 11 to 14 days while her mate feeds her on the nest. Both parents feed the young, which are out of the nest and flying in a couple of weeks, allowing the parents to recycle and produce a second brood before the family has to fly south at the end of summer.

ATTRACTED TO:
shrubbery, ground cover, vines, brush piles, feeders, water, insects

SONG SPARROW

Sometime in mid-March, when the ears are starved for the sounds of spring, a song sparrow will mount the tallest lilac in the garden and proclaim the end of winter with a beautiful *sweet, sweet, sweet—as ever it may be.*

Such a lovely song comes from a rather plain brown bird with a heavily streaked breast featuring a large central breast spot. Yet, the appearance of the song sparrow is greatly enhanced by its sprightly spirit—standing on tiptoes, tail flicking, and much scurrying in and out beneath the shrubbery like chipmunks.

Populations of song sparrows are as widespread as any garden birds in America. So widespread, in fact, that they show regional differences in size, color, and song. In other words, the song sparrows in the South seem to have a distinct southern accent, as compared to their relatives that live in the North. These populations are considered permanent residents of the regions in which they live, though many of those in the North move toward the South in winter, and return to the North early in the spring.

During the time that song sparrows are proclaiming the new season, they frequent gardens where waste seeds have been spilled from bird feeders. But as the spring moves on, they become inconspicuous as the paired birds turn to the domestic duties of building nests and raising young.

These ground-inhabiting birds usually build their well-hidden nests on the ground, under low bushes. The nests of grasses, rootlets and leaves are built by the female, who then lays three to five heavily spotted, greenish eggs. Song sparrows will often raise a brown-headed cowbird youngster after a female cowbird removes a song sparrow egg from the nest and replaces it with one of her own. If all goes well, the song sparrow pair can raise several broods a year.

ATTRACTED TO:
shrubbery, ground cover, vines, brush piles, feeders, water, insects

HOUSE SPARROW

terrible commotion resounded in the garden. A pair of house sparrows was attacking a pair of bluebirds at the birdhouse. The bluebirds had been carrying grasses into the house where they would lay eggs and raise youngsters. But the house sparrows had a different plan for the house, entering it time and again, removing the grasses that the bluebirds had carried into it.

Despite the angry calls of the bluebirds, and their attempts to defend the birdhouse as their own, the house sparrows eventually drove the bluebirds away. The house sparrows went on to lay their own set of five eggs and raise the hatchlings.

Such is the role of house sparrows in North America ever since they were introduced from Europe over a century ago. In finding their niche, they have aggressively displaced native birds from nesting and feeding locations across the continent. They reached the height of their population density in North America when horses were the principle form of transportation, gleaning a great deal of their food supply from the residue of horse food.

House sparrows are noisy, chattering birds that twitter and chip most of the time but have no real song. In fact, they are not true sparrows, but members of the weaver finch family, a fact that becomes more evident when their nests are studied. House sparrows will nest in any birdhouse, natural cavity, rafter, hole in a wall, billboard support, awning, behind shutters and any other nooks and crannies of buildings. The nests they build inside are huge balls of grass, weeds and trash.

Yet, for some city gardeners, house sparrows are the only birds they see and entertain, and despite their proclivities for ousting native birds, house sparrows have strong family bonds, making them interesting birds to watch.

ATTRACTED TO:
small trees, shrubbery, buildings, feeders, birdhouse

HOUSE FINCH

ntil government agents raided a pet shop on Long Island in the 1940s, house finches were strictly western birds. But an illegal attempt to make them cage birds backfired when the Long Island pet store owner released the captives to avoid being arrested. Since then, house finches have spread from New York throughout the East and the Midwest, where they reportedly reunited with their western relatives at the Missouri River in 1988.

Today, house finches are among the commonest of all garden birds throughout the continent. The orange-red on the head, bib and rump of males causes some Easterners to confuse them with purple finches, whose red is more raspberry-colored. The females of both species are brown-striped, but the house finch females are lighter and softer striped, and their bodies are slimmer, more streamlined than those of their purple finch cousins.

House finches have adapted so well to living around houses and in gardens that they often nest under eaves, above doors, and in hanging flower pots, especially those containing geraniums. In the middle of the flowers, the house finches build their nest, lay four or five eggs, and nurture the youngsters until they can fly. The geraniums don't seem to mind.

Both males and females sing lovely canarylike warbling songs and carry on a continuous sweet *queet* chatter among themselves all day long. House finches are very social birds, and after the nesting season, they merge into family and extended family flocks for the remainder of the year. At feeders, they are fond of niger (thistle) seeds, as well as sunflower seeds in any form. They also spend a great deal of time at birdbaths.

ATTRACTED TO:
small trees, shrubbery, buildings, feeders, water

PURPLE FINCH

Like a living ornament on a Christmas tree, a male purple finch perching on an evergreen tree decorates a garden in winter as few other birds can. He has been described as "a sparrow dipped in raspberry juice."

Unfortunately, these lovely birds visit gardens only in winter, and only when their natural food of tree seeds in northern coniferous forests is in short supply. But during those winters, large flocks of purple finches will descend on garden bird feeders containing sunflower and niger (thistle) seeds, as far south as the Deep South and the Southwest.

Yet, with the large number of house finches now visiting gardens in winter, one must look closely to be certain which bird one is seeing. Purple finches are chunkier than house finches, and the males are deeper red, or raspberry. Female purple finches are darker and more heavily streaked than their house finch counterparts.

During warm months, purple finches are paired and build well-concealed nests on a horizontal branch of a conifer, sometimes as high as 60 feet above the ground. It is during the nesting season that purple finches eat insects, fruits and berries. Their rich, musical, canarylike song rises and falls, sometimes given while flying, often repeated. Their call or alarm note is a quick *pick* or *puck* sound.

It appears that fewer purple finches are being seen at garden feeders since house finches have become so common. Perhaps the competition for feeder food from the more aggressive house finches has made purple finches shier, if not scarcer. Yet any gardener who would like to attract purple finches in winter may be able to do so by offering sunflower seeds near evergreens.

ATTRACTED TO:
tall trees, small trees, shrubbery, feeders, water

AMERICAN GOLDFINCH

ike a Monet painting come to life, a band of bright yellow goldfinches swoops down on a prairie field of bull thistles, Queen Anne's lace and purple coneflowers. It is late July, the time of American goldfinches—the last birds to nest in summer. They have been waiting for the thistles to mature, as they use the thistle down to build their nests and the seeds to feed their young.

No American garden is complete without its band of goldfinches, the wild canaries of North America. Their bright and cheerful presence, and their *per-chick-a-ree* calls uttered with each undulation of flight, is part and parcel of summer flower gardens. In winter, their *see-me* calls and light-hearted behavior at garden feeders give hope for the coming spring.

Actually, goldfinches are living forecasters of the changing seasons. In late summer, the bright canary yellow males begin to change to olive brown long before cold weather arrives . . . the first sign of fall. Their complete change to winter plumage is so dramatic that some people believe they are two totally different kinds of birds. Likewise, in deep winter, the first bright yellow spots begin to appear on the olive brown males, giving them a "blotched" appearance; a sure sign that spring is near.

When spring does arrive, goldfinches are all dressed up in their finest yellow with no place to go. They must wait for the thistle to bloom before they can raise their five young on regurgitated, partially digested seeds, called "canary milk."

These social birds remain together in loose bands throughout the year, making them excellent year-round feeder birds. They are fond of niger (thistle) seeds and sunflower seeds in any form, offered in hanging tube feeders. Water for drinking and bathing is also a big attraction for goldfinches.

ATTRACTED TO:
tall trees, small trees, shrubbery, fields, feeders, water

PINE SISKIN

he invasion was on! There were so many pine siskins on feeders that there was no space left for dozens more hungry birds that wanted to feed. Like honey bees swarming around combs, some 60 heavily brown-streaked siskins vied for perches at the tube feeders, hour after hour, throughout the cold, steel-gray wintry day in February. Yet, despite the cold, the siskins seemed hot as they squabbled, attacked, challenged and threatened each other for a place at the dinner table.

It is estimated that these were among, at the very least, 95 million pine siskins at feeders throughout the continent during that recent winter, a 99 percent increase over the number that visited feeders the previous year.

Pine siskins are traveling birds . . . gypsies from the North. They are known for staging massive invasions to all corners of North America, as far south as the Gulf Coast, when the conifer trees in the boreal forests where they live fail to produce an adequate crop of seeds. The so-called irruptions occur periodically when the population of siskins are high and their food supplies low. Otherwise, pine siskins are rarely seen at backyard and garden bird feeders in the lower 48 states.

When they do invade, they remain for most of the winter. But as they near their time for leaving, their spring song, an insectlike, buzzing trill that rises in pitch, transcends the garden.

Then, in huge flocks, they migrate back to the North, where they build concealed nests on horizontal branches of the same coniferous trees that produce their natural food. In pairs, in loose colonies, the siskins raise three to four youngsters each, and if most nests are successful, the population will boom again, perhaps causing another invasion south.

ATTRACTED TO:
tall trees, small trees, shrubbery, feeders, water

SCARLET TANAGER

otally exhausted, the brilliantly colored male scarlet tanager sat motionless on the ground among the fresh green leaves and dried brown twigs.

This reddest of all redbirds, with black wings and tail, had just crossed Lake Erie and made landfall at the very tip of Canada, at Point Pelee National Park. Some days or weeks before, it had left its wintering grounds in South America. And the crash landing at Point Pelee probably wasn't the end of this tanager's flight, as the bird would most likely be back in the sky in a few hours, heading farther north into Canada to establish a breeding territory. A few days later, a dull, green-backed female, yellow below with blackish wings and tail, would arrive on the same territory to begin the pair's nesting season.

Of all the beautiful garden birds in North America, the male scarlet tanager, during the breeding season, is at the top of the list. Yet, despite its brilliant scarlet color, it is a shy bird that hides in the foliage of thick deciduous and coniferous trees, and is heard singing a caroling *queer-it, queeer, queer-it, queer* song that sounds like a robin with a sore throat. The female, whose colors help her blend into the forest habitat, is also shy, and may be noticed only when she gives the *chip-churr* alarm call.

Scarlet tanagers are also very secretive about the location of their nest of twigs, on a tree branch 8 to 75 feet above the ground, where they raise three to five youngsters.

Before migrating south in late summer, the male molts his red feathers for yellow.

Scarlet tanagers will visit garden pools to bathe and drink, and may eat bird cakes of cornmeal, peanut butter and beef suet at feeders.

ATTRACTED TO:
*tall trees, shrubbery,
feeders, water, insects*

WESTERN TANAGER

n important part of setting up camp in the West is putting out cups of sugar water for the hummingbirds. But the first visitor at the sugar water at Madera Canyon in Arizona was a male western tanager. A few minutes later, there were six male western tanagers lined up waiting to take their turns at the sugar water.

Among the most striking garden birds in the West, male western tanagers have a red head and face, yellow body, and black wings with prominent bars. Usually shy birds of the treetops, these western tanagers had learned from experience that the sugar water was free to any bird that showed itself. After a few more minutes, a dull olive-green female arrived to take her turn at the sweet water.

Aside from being attracted to gardens in the western mountains that offer sugar water, western tanagers will also stop for a bath and drink in pools and garden springs. The male's hoarse robinlike song may be heard from the tops of coniferous trees from the time they arrive back in the North from their wintering grounds in Mexico and Central America in April and May until they are ready to return there in late summer.

While the males sing, the females are busy building compact saucer nests in the forks of horizontal branches of pines, firs or oaks, some 20 to 30 feet above the ground. Each will lay three to five bluish green eggs, and incubate them alone for 13 days. Both parents feed the youngsters. Because the summers are so short in the tanager's mountain habitat, they raise only one brood a year.

Yet, western tanagers seem not to be in a hurry to migrate, and may loiter in gardens of the High West where they are being fed.

ATTRACTED TO:
tall trees, shrubbery,
feeders, water, insects

MEADOWLARK

Standing tall on the top of a fence post, a male meadowlark raises its head to the sky and declares, *spring-of-the-year.* And with that simple, melodious call, the bird with a black *V* across its bright yellow breast announces the change of seasons in the East.

This is an eastern meadowlark, which is not a lark, but a member of the blackbird family, along with bobolinks, orioles and redwings. Had the bird with a black V across its bright yellow breast announced the change of seasons with a bubbling, flute-like song, it would have been a western meadowlark proclaiming spring in the West. The two meadowlarks are identical except for their very different songs. Neither bird migrates farther south in winter than the southern United States, which allows them to be among the first to return to their breeding grounds in early March.

These birds of meadows, prairies and open fields may frequent gardens in search of insects or seeds when gardens are nearby. Like bluebirds and red-winged blackbirds, meadowlarks may trade back and forth between their nesting habitat and feeding habitats in gardens.

When searching for food, meadowlarks walk, not hop like many other birds, as they wind their way through dense grasses. When they fly, they use a fluttering flap, soar, flap, soar motion to propel them low across grassy fields.

Female meadowlarks, identical in appearance to the males, are secretive birds that build carefully hidden grassy nests, domed over the top, to conceal their three to five eggs from predatory eyes. Young meadowlarks are fed entirely on insects carried to them by their mothers. To approach the nest, the female lands in the grass some distance away, and then walks on a well worn path the rest of the way to the nest.

ATTRACTED TO:
open fields, insects

BALTIMORE ORIOLE

he bright orange and black bird with white wing bars streaks across the patio and lands on the sugar water feeder. The male Baltimore oriole's weight on the perch lowers the cover over the feeder port, allowing the handsome bird to sip its fill of the sweet fluid.

The oriole feeder is a breakthrough in bird feeding that allows people to enjoy the spectacular birds throughout their spring and summer visit in North America. Orioles always seemed to be interested in hummingbird feeders, but because the feeders were designed to accommodate hummingbirds, not orioles, the larger birds could not easily drink from them. Orioles had to be enticed with orange halves, but the birds' interest in the citrus juices seems to wane in early summer, about the time they are feeding young in the nest. The sugar water feeders for orioles appear to hold the orioles' interest throughout the season, up to the time they migrate south in early autumn.

The feeder is visited by both sexes, but not as often by the drab-colored female when she is incubating eggs in her skillfully woven, deep, pouchlike nest. The nest, hanging from the end of a branch some 6 to 60 feet above the ground, is difficult to see, but when the youngsters become vocal, demanding ever more food from their parents, they draw attention to the nest, making it easier to find.

The male's striking colors are reason enough to make the Baltimore oriole a favorite garden bird, but its liquid flutelike song provides another good reason to keep it nearby with sugar water.

Named for having the same colors as those in the livery of the first Baron of Baltimore, a colonizer of Maryland, the Baltimore oriole is a member of the North American family of blackbirds.

ATTRACTED TO:
tall trees, feeders, water, sugar water, fruit, insects

RED-WINGED BLACKBIRD

Like a messenger from the land of green fields and flowering trees, the first male red-winged blackbird arrives during the first week of March at garden bird feeders in the North. Lifting his head toward the steel-gray sky, and spreading his wings to show off scarlet epaulettes, the redwing announces the advent of spring with a gurgling *kong-ga-ree.*

Surely this new arrival noticed the frozen lake, the cattail marsh knee-deep in snow, and the spitting of flurries that portends more winter in the offing.

Yet, the redwing persists, trading back and forth from the feeders to the nearby marsh where it stakes a claim to a few square yards of frozen cattails, defined by invisible boundaries, fending off other males that arrive in the area. In a few more days, the males are joined by the brown-striped females, who take up residence in the harems of the mates of their choosing.

As time passes and that first redwing has proved that spring was inevitable, the females build grassy nests in newly sprouted cattail shoots, or in the midst of grassy fields. They alone incubate the eggs, and raise the youngsters without any help from their mates.

Meanwhile, the males continue to run each other off territories, but are surprisingly amicable at garden feeders. Apparently, these colonial nesters consider feeding grounds neutral. Also, surprisingly, very few if any females visit feeders during the nesting season, as feeders seem to be the dining rooms of avian men's clubs.

Red-winged blackbirds frequent garden feeders and baths until late summer, when the shortening hours of daylight cause them to gather into large flocks in preparation for the return flight to southern climes for winter.

ATTRACTED TO:
wetlands, feeders, water, insects

EASTERN BLUEBIRD

Gardeners searching for signs of spring in March revel when a flash of blue lands on a fence post, flits a wing, and warbles a soft, melodious *tru-al-lee.* The male bluebird has arrived, and so has spring.

Perched erect, the male eastern bluebird wears the velvet blue of the sky on its back and the reddish-brown of the earth on its breast. The female, who arrives a few days later, is a paler version of the male.

Together, they select a nesting site in a tree cavity, old woodpecker hole or birdhouse located at the edge of a garden or field. Into the cavity they carry dry grasses to fashion a loosely arranged nest. The female lays four or five pale blue eggs, and then incubates them for about two weeks until they hatch. Meanwhile, the male often carries food to the female inside the house while she is tending the eggs. Both parents feed the hatchlings a variety of insects for about three weeks, until the youngsters are on their own.

Two broods a year are common among bluebirds, and sometimes the young from the first nesting help their parents feed the second brood.

In pursuit of their insect diet, bluebirds often flutter to the ground and then back to a perch on a fence post or wire with their prey. At garden feeders, bluebirds may eat fruits, berries or mealworms. They also enjoy a dip and a drink at the birdbath. But the best way to guarantee a bluebird summer is to put up birdhouses on posts at the edge of the garden or nearby open field.

The other two North American bluebirds are the western, with a patch of brick-red between its shoulders, and the mountain, with a blue back, light blue breast and white belly.

ATTRACTED TO:
open fields, feeders, water, fruit, insects, birdhouse

Wood Thrush

er-al-deeeen. As the flutelike liquid notes of a wood thrush herald the dawning of a new day, the dew-drenched woodland surrounding the garden becomes a cathedral where prayers of thanksgiving may be given for a bird song so beautiful. There are bird songs . . . and then there is the dawn chorus of the wood thrush, possibly the most beautiful music in all of nature.

Their caroling aside, wood thrushes are quiet birds that come and go on silent wings from gardens to damp woodland thickets, only occasionally uttering a rapid *pit, pit, pit* alarm note. A closer look reveals a handsome rusty-brown back, a brighter reddish-brown head, and a heavily dotted white breast. Males and females look alike.

Follow the wood thrush pair and you might be led to their nest of mud, leaves and the occasional scrap of paper, firmly anchored and well hidden in the crotch of a small tree or shrub. Look into it and admire the three or four pale blue-green eggs. Return days later and delight at the stubby-tailed miniatures of their parents, as the brood prepares to fledge.

Wood thrushes arrive in the eastern and central states in late April and May from winter retreats in Central America. In search of insects, wood thrushes will visit gardens during migration and throughout the spring and early summer in and near their established nesting territories. They may also be tempted by bird feeders that offer fruit or bird cakes containing corn meal, peanut butter and beef suet.

The singing chorus of wood thrushes ends all too soon as the season advances and spring green deepens to late summer's sylvan maturity. It will be many months before the gardener is again heard saying. "Listen, there's a wood thrush song. Isn't it lovely?"

ATTRACTED TO:
*tall trees, shrubbery,
water, fruit, insects*

AMERICAN ROBIN

**L**ike a swarm of bees, a congregation of American robins, hundreds of them, mill around a lawn sprayer, fluttering wings and tails, preening with yellow bills, each bird bathing and grooming its feathers for another day of flight.

It is winter in Florida, a time when flocks of robins tour southern gardens in search of earthworms, insects and fruit, and wait out the season.

Yet, as the minutes of daylight increase with each passing day, the robins become restless. Then one day a signal is given inside each robin . . . a signal to head north . . . north with the spring . . . north to the breeding grounds in yards and gardens across America.

The males go first. They must establish a territory, and defend it against all other males, even the robin they see in the reflection of a window and or the rear-view mirror of a parked car.

Then the females head north in search of perfect males with the best territories, where there are plenty of earthworms, and lots of insects, berries and other fruits, abundant natural cover, and places to build nests, lay sky blue eggs and raise youngsters with spotted breasts, perhaps twice, if all goes well.

A female in flight hears a male's caroling *cheer-o-lee, cheer-up, cheer-o-lee, cheer-up* song. She stops and considers his song, his territory, his appearance. This is the place for her. She responds to the handsome male with his slate gray back, darker gray head, and brick-red breast.

Soon, she is building a nest of mud and grass. Sometimes she seems unsure, so she builds another nest, and then still others, sometimes side by side. Finally she settles on the first nest, and lays four eggs. And so goes the life cycle of the American robin, the continent's most popular garden bird.

ATTRACTED TO:
*tall trees, shrubbery,
water, fruit, insects*

GRAY CATBIRD

Pity the poor gardener that hasn't left a corner of the yard in dense shrubbery for the sake of the gray catbird. This shy, dark gray bird with a black cap and dark red under the tail more than makes up for its plain appearance with a musical score that is comical, fascinating, and imitative.

Named for its catlike *mew*, that is usually given in alarm, the true song of the male gray catbird is quite different, a lively series of unrelated and often disjointed musical notes and phrases. Not only does one hear the odd yowl of a cat, and the guttural remarks of a frog, but the squeegee of a window wiper and the calls and whistles of other bird notes, all of which create a unique mix of catbird cacophony. One astute listener suggested that the catbird "sings Chinese."

When one considers that the gray catbird is a close relative to the northern mockingbird and brown thrasher, all that noise makes some sense.

The object of those delightful noises, the female catbird, takes up residence in that odd corner of tangle, where she builds a bulky nest of twigs, vines, and leaves, into which she lays four bluish-green eggs. While she is busy with domestic responsibilities, her mate charms with his conglomeration of notes, phrases and calls.

When one glimpses a catbird, its actions appear quick and jerky as it darts here and there on running legs, tail ever flicking.

Because a catbird's diet is half insects and half fruits and berries, the best way to keep the vagabond songster around is with a garden pool, where a bath and drink of fresh water are readily available.

That specialized diet is the reason why catbirds must leave northern gardens in late summer to take up residence in more tropical environs for the winter.

ATTRACTED TO:
shrubbery, vines, brush piles, sugar water, fruit, insects, water

Northern Mockingbird

homas, the orange tabby, slinks across the lawn, past the garden and toward the hedge. Just as he is about to enter the thicket, a gray feathered projectile rifles down out of the magnolia tree and clobbers Thomas a mighty whack on the head.

Totally bewildered, and caught by surprise, Thomas beats a quick retreat toward the security of the house, only to be hit again and again by two balls of gray and white feathers amidst the clatter of loud *tchack!* alarm calls.

Once again, Thomas has been attacked by the pair of northern mockingbirds with whom he supposedly shares a backyard and garden. Yet, since the mockers built their bulky nest in the hedge, there has been no sharing of the garden with Thomas.

Despite their aggressive behavior toward predators, northern mockingbirds are delightful birds to have around. What they lack in beauty, they more than make up for in song and dramatic display.

Aptly described by John Burroughs as "the lark and the nightingale in one," the mockingbird has an endless repertoire of calls, many of which mimic the songs of other birds. This "mock-bird," as the early colonists called it, or *Cencontlatolly*, bird of four-hundred tongues, as native Americans dubbed it, is reported to have changed its tune 310 times in 15 minutes, interspersing 114 notes and phrases of 29 other birds. It is also well-known for singing all night long by the light of a full moon, edging some insomniacs to the point of desperation.

Northern mockingbirds may be as southern as pecan pie, but in recent years, they have expanded their ranges to the point of now being All-American birds. Gardeners who feed mockingbirds seeds and fruits year-round are without a dull moment of bird watching.

ATTRACTED TO:
shrubbery, vines, brush piles, sugar water, fruit, insects, water

Brown Thrasher

ts angry-looking yellow eye betrays the brown thrasher's personality. Approach its nest on the ground or in low-growing shrubbery and the bird will indeed attack and may even strike you on the head with its long curved-down bill. Yet left alone, it is a rather shy bird of the garden edges and thickets, quietly going about its business.

The only time that brown thrashers are obviously in residence in the garden area is when the male sings his loud and boisterous song, *hit it, hit it; watch out, watch out; not me, not me*. If you approach their bulky nest with its four eggs or young, both birds will sound their alarm note, a loud *smak*.

Brown thrashers and their close relatives, mockingbirds and catbirds, are members of the family of birds known as mimic thrushes because their songs often mimic the songs of other birds. Brown thrashers occasionally mimic other birds, but more often they create their own noisy notes that are always repeated. Gardeners familiar with mockingbirds may call a brown thrasher a "brown mockingbird."

"I have a brown thrush in my garden," is another common misnomer, because the brown thrasher has the same bright reddish-brown back as the wood thrush, though the thrasher's breast is streaked, not spotted, as the wood thrush's.

Gardens frequented by brown thrashers will benefit from some insect control, as 65 percent of their summer diet is insects. They may also eat salamanders, small snakes, lizards and frogs, plus a variety of fruit during late summer.

As the summer wanes, and young brown thrashers are on the wing, the striking foxy-brown birds with long tails, striped breasts, and yellow eyes will move leisurely toward the Southeast to establish a winter feeding territory where berries and insects will be abundant.

ATTRACTED TO:
shrubbery, vines, brush piles, sugar water, fruit, insects, water

TREE SWALLOW

"**E**very time I put up a bluebird house, I get tree swallows nesting in it," complained a neighbor. "What can I do about it?" he asked.

"Consider yourself fortunate to have tree swallows nesting in your garden," is the best response.

So highly valued was one house full of young tree swallows, that when it was vandalized by some insensitive boys, the owner gathered up the four surviving youngsters from the ground, placed them in a new birdhouse in the same location, and called the local television station to tell the story of what happened. Fortunately, the swallow parents accepted the new house, and resumed their feeding of the young. A week later, the four survivors flew out of the house, and presumably lived happily ever after.

Tree swallows are somewhat different from other members of the swallow family. They are colonial in nature only during migration and while on their winter feeding grounds in the southern United States. When nesting, they often prefer living in isolated pairs. Also, they traditionally build nests in tree cavities, such as abandoned woodpecker holes. That is why they will readily accept birdhouses as nesting sites, and return to the same garden locations year after year.

Like bluebirds, tree swallows will respond positively to efforts to establish birdhouse trails, and will fill any number of new nesting houses as they are placed on fence posts in rural areas, particularly near water.

Because their diets are largely insectivorous, tree swallows, like purple martins, are subject to starvation when cold snaps deplete their insect food supplies.

Tree swallows can be aggressive when it comes to the possession of a nesting house. Yet, their graceful flight, on steely blue-green wings, and their quiet *silip* call as they glide through a garden in search of insects make it well worth having these lovely birds around.

ATTRACTED TO:
open fields, water, insects, birdhouse

PURPLE MARTIN

A single bluish-black bird lands on the purple martin house 20 feet above the garden. Then another one lands, and another. As each new bird appears, it gives a gurgling, liquid call to announce its arrival.

This is the first week of April, and the advance guard of several male purple martins is arriving from its wintering grounds in South America. Like other swallows returning to more famous destinations in North America, the arrival date of a purple martin colony varies only a few days every spring.

The scouts are joined days later by the main flock of the colony, which may number in the hundreds. The birds have been en route north for weeks, and finally reach their destination, the garden habitat in which they were hatched. The purple martins' summer has just begun.

Of all garden birds, perhaps none is more enthusiastically welcomed each spring than purple martins. During the winter, the apartment house containing two dozen nesting rooms was cleaned, painted, and now remounted on a pole in anticipation of the advanced guard's arrival. The only concern now is that a late spring storm or cold snap doesn't destroy the insects upon which the martins depend for their survival. There have been years when such catastrophes have occurred, and the colony has been devastated by starvation.

Not this year, as each blue-black male and his dingy-colored mate select a room in the house and begin carrying in nesting materials. When their brood hatches, each of the four to five youngsters will require a huge food supply of insects that the parents will capture from the garden area. During a purple martin's summer, the number of flying insects consumed by the colony is immense, thus placing much value on these elegant birds.

ATTRACTED TO:
open fields, water, insects, birdhouse

Barn Swallow

When colonists from Europe first noticed a bird that looked and acted like a bird they knew at home as the swallow, they called it the swallow. But, there were other swallows in America, so they distinguished this one by naming it the barn swallow because of its obvious attraction to barns. As it turned out, the barn swallow actually is the same species as the one and only swallow in Europe.

Today, there are very few barns, garden sheds, and other outbuildings in rural America that don't have at least one nesting pair of barn swallows during summer months. And most farmers and gardeners regard them as helpers in the difficult task of controlling insect pests.

In addition, barn swallows are lovely fork-tailed birds with metallic blue-black backs, cinnamon breasts and bellies, and darker reddish-brown throats. They are constantly chattering *kittick, kittick, kittick* as they dart around fields and gardens consuming flying insects, providing seasonal music for the enjoyment of all who listen.

Insect populations are further depleted when barn swallow pairs produce four to six youngsters which require a steady diet of the same kinds of garden pests. Imagine the insect control that 55 swallow nests produced on one farm in Pennsylvania!

But before that happens, a barn swallow pair must fashion an artistic cuplike nest plastered to rafters, eaves or beams with balls of mud they carry in their bills. They line each nest with chicken feathers. Here they raise two broods a summer, and often repeat the cycle in the same nesting site, year after year.

Barn swallows, like their purple martin relatives, arrive in the North each spring within a week or so of the same date. When the season is over, large flocks of family groups return to Mexico, Central and South America where they spend the winters.

ATTRACTED TO:
open fields, water, insects, buildings

CLIFF SWALLOW

Those are "eaves swallows," the old farmer insisted. "They have been nesting under the eaves of that barn since my grandfather built it 100 years ago," he said.

It is true that the cliff swallow might be better named if it were called eaves swallow, and many people call it that. But the correct name for these interesting and beneficial birds is cliff swallow, because in undeveloped areas they still nest on the sides of cliffs.

These days, most cliff swallows, like barn swallows, seek barns, sheds, garages, park pavilions, and other outbuildings where they build their nests under the eaves. Cliff swallows are even more sociable than barn swallows, and live together in large colonies, building their nests side-by-side.

Cliff swallow nests are, perhaps, the most interesting aspect of this bird. Gathering balls of mud in their bills from nearby puddles and stream banks, cliff swallows carry them to the nesting site. There they will shape bottlelike nests from the inside out from the mud balls mixed with straw, just like the adobe used by some native Americans to build their homes in the arid Southwest. The birds then line their nests with feathers. When completed, the nests are totally enclosed except for an entrance hole in the front.

Cliff swallows are the farmer's and gardener's friends because their diets consist entirely of insects. And when every nest in the colony has three to six youngsters in it, the number of insects consumed by the birds in a single day is astronomical.

Cliff swallows sometimes nest near barn swallows, but the two birds may be differentiated by the shape of their tails—the cliff's is wedged, while the barn's is forked. In addition, there is a buffy rump patch on the cliff swallow.

Because cliff swallows can't survive without insects to eat, they spend the winter as far south as Argentina.

ATTRACTED TO:
open fields, water, insects, buildings

GREATER ROADRUNNER

The roadrunner cartoon character, a chickenlike bird that is mostly tail, feet and head that speeds down the highway calling *beep, beep,* and outwits coyotes, is actually based on fact.

A pair of roadrunners in New Mexico was observed as they appeared to enjoy being chased by a hound that could never catch them. This real-life cartoon went on day after day, as the birds had no problem keeping well ahead of their pursuer without having to fly.

The real roadrunner is as delightful a bird as the one depicted in the cartoon. "To get to know a roadrunner," according to Dr. George M. Sutton, a biologist who studied the birds, "you have to watch him race across the sand, full speed, after a lizard ... watch him put out his wing, change course, throw up his tail, change his course again, plunge headlong into a clump of cactus, and emerge, whacking his limp victim on the ground."

This beloved, respected and amusing bird is a symbol of the desert and the State Bird of New Mexico. Yet, it lives throughout the Southwest, and as far east as Arkansas, Louisiana, and Missouri. Its taste for lizards and snakes makes it a very welcome bird in any garden.

Native Americans thought the roadrunner had special powers because its toes form an X print; the Spanish call it *paisano,* fellow countryman.

Roadrunner pairs appear to have a strong attachment to each other and are bonded for life. Their courtship consists of much flicking and wagging of their tails, chasing, and offering of sticks and other gifts.

Like the cartoon character, the real roadrunner is noisy, but the male's song is a *coo, coo, coo, ooh, ooh, ooh, ooh, ooh.* And both birds purr.

ATTRACTED TO:
*small trees, shrubbery,
vines, insects*

EASTERN PHOEBE

 hoebes seem to like people and people certainly like phoebes. They are very plain birds, with brown-gray above and white below, and the sexes are exactly alike in appearance. Yet, they do have two distinguishing habits: constantly bobbing their tails, and repeatedly calling their name: *FEE-bee* or *fee-BEE*.

Lucky is the gardener who has a phoebe nesting above the door of the potting shed, for these birds are both helpful and friendly. As members of the flycatcher family, their diets consist almost entirely of insects. Imagine having two living insect traps working overtime everyday to keep the garden free of flying insects, and requiring no wages.

The most enticing feature of these birds is where they build their large, well constructed nests. Invariably, phoebes use a ledge, rafter or shelf, often near water, but beyond that they may build in some peculiar places. Many construct under bridges; others under the eaves of a house, shed or barn; still others like the flat walls of a cliff or the entrance to a cave or mine. One pair built a nest on the top of a cabin bell year after year, another on the top of an electric meter in a youth camp. Still another selected a ledge under a patio deck, allowing a view down into the nest through the floor planks. And once they are successful, they seem to return to the same location year after year.

Regardless of where they nest, they always have a favorite perch near the nest, from which they fly out, snap up a flying insect, and then dart back to the perch. When they bring food to the nestlings, they invariably land on the perch first, check to see if it is safe, then fly to the nest carrying the insect food in their bills.

ATTRACTED TO:
water, insects, buildings

RUBY-THROATED HUMMINGBIRD

he dominant male ruby-throated hummingbird at the sugar water feeder is Guardbird. He decides who will eat there and who will not. Other male rubythroats that attempt to feed are dive-bombed and quickly chased away. Only the loyal female members of Guardbird's harem are allowed to sip all the sugar water their pudgy little tummies can hold.

All this hummingbird activity begins in the garden when Guardbird arrives back from his wintering grounds in Central and South America sometime in early May. If the sugar water feeders are not up yet, he will hover at the exact spot where they were hanging last summer. If that doesn't produce feeders, he may fly up to the window, and look inside as if asking, "Where are the feeders?"

Soon after the females arrive, the grandest of hummingbird shows begins when Guardbird goes-a-courting. Taking a shine to a particular female rubythroat, Guardbird tries to get her attention by zipping up into the sky, and then diving in front of her at 60 miles per hour in a wide pendulum swing. Seemingly oblivious to his gyrations, the female quietly preens her feathers as if nothing is happening.

Not only is Guardbird colorful with his emerald green back and flashing ruby throat, but he is relatively noisy. His wings make a buzzing sound as they beat 75 times a second, and he is constantly vocalizing as he fills the air with high-pitched squeaky chipperings.

After he has bred each of the females in his harem, Guardbird's domestic duties are completed. It is the responsibility of a female to fashion a tiny nest and raise two youngsters. Yet, when the youngsters have fledged and join the adults at the feeders, Guardbird seems to know they are his offspring and usually does not chase them away.

ATTRACTED TO:
tall trees, small trees, sugar water, flowers, insects

ANNA'S HUMMINGBIRD

Traditionally a resident of the West Coast, Anna's hummingbirds will occasionally stray eastward. One Anna's was really lost when it was spotted drinking sugar water at a feeder in Milwaukee, Wisconsin.

Word of the bird spread, and it soon became a big attraction for hummingbird enthusiasts in the Midwest. But concern replaced delight when autumn winds began to blow and all the ruby-throated hummingbirds had migrated south.

When it became apparent that the Anna's wasn't going to leave before winter set in, a local bird bander caught the tiny mite and delivered it to the domed botanical gardens in Milwaukee where it was released in the tropical display. A sugar water feeder was set up and the Anna's spent the cold Wisconsin winter inside, in tropical habitat, with plenty to eat. When spring arrived, the hummingbird was transported by airplane to California where it was released.

California is home for Anna's, particularly in gardens and parks where it can find nectar in flowers and sugar water in feeders. The male Anna's is marked with a rose-red crown and throat patch. His courtship flights are wild affairs in which he climbs high in the sky and then dives straight down toward the female. As he nears her, he spreads his tail feathers, puts on his breaks, and utters a soft *peek* in her ear.

The female is mostly green on the back and white below to camouflage her as she incubates two white, bean-sized eggs for about 16 days. When the youngsters leave the nest at about three weeks of age and join the adults at feeders, they look like females, but with shorter tails.

In addition to a fondness for sugar water, Anna's are attracted to gardens where bee balm, coral bells, and honeysuckle grow near natural habitat.

ATTRACTED TO:
tall trees, small trees, sugar water, flowers, insects

BROAD-TAILED HUMMINGBIRD

Summer residents in tourist cabins at Rocky Mountain National Park, Colorado, are hooked on feeding broad-tailed humming-birds. Even the first-timers soon rush to the local hardware store in Estes Park to buy feeders and sugar water when they see how easily their neighbors feed the broadtails outside their back doors.

Like swarms of bees, the broadtails whiz back and forth between cabins, a sip here and a sip there, and then zip off to the next one, all day long.

Eastern visitors may notice how much like male ruby-throated hummingbirds are the male broadtails with their bright red throats, metallic green backs and white bellies. Likewise, the females are metallic green above and white below.

Like all hummingbirds, the broadtails can fly frontwards, backwards, straight up, and straight down. But the broadwings are distinguished from other hummingbirds by the loud buzzing sound made by their wings.

Male broadtails return to the Rocky Mountains from Mexico and Guatemala in spring, ahead of the females, to establish territories. When the females arrive, the males perform an array of dazzling courtship flights that begin and end where the female is perched.

The female builds a neat little cup nest of plant down, decorated with tiny pieces of bark, leaves and plant fibers. She then lays two tiny white eggs, which she alone incubates for about two weeks. The youngsters are spitting images of her when they leave the nest.

In addition to sugar water, broadtails will sip nectar from a variety of garden flowers, including red geraniums, lupines and petunias. They also seek nectar from a variety of native high country wildflowers.

ATTRACTED TO:
tall trees, small trees, sugar water, flowers, insects

Yellow Warbler

weet, sweet, sweet, I'm so sweet, sings the yellow warbler male from the garden shrubbery. Indeed he is sweet, for yellow warblers and summer garden flowers mix and match as well as any natural combination imaginable.

The all-yellow canarylike birds, sometimes called "yellow summer birds," bring motion and sound to garden sites throughout the continent, as yellow warblers are the most widespread of all warblers in North America.

But they must be enjoyed quickly, for they arrive during apple blossom time and are already on their way back to Mexico, the Caribbean and Central and South America by the time the thistledown flies in mid-summer.

Though yellow warblers set up independent nesting territories, they may share the garden with a number of other pairs in loose colonies, such as in a large planting of multi-flora rose where nests may be only a few yards apart.

But hurried though they may be, no other warbler builds as neat and as compact a nest as the yellow warbler. Placing the nest in the upright fork of a shrub, tree or brier, the birds use milkweed fibers, plant down and fine grasses, perhaps some hair, to construct a dense silver cup. The egg-laying process of one egg a day may be interrupted by a brown-headed cowbird, which will remove one warbler egg and replace it with her own. Yet yellow warblers are intolerant of cowbird parasitization, and may build a second story on the nest to bury the cowbird eggs. As many as six stories have been added to a single yellow warbler nest in defense against cowbird eggs.

Garden shrubbery is not the only attraction for yellow warblers. They may also spend considerable time drinking and bathing in garden birdbaths.

ATTRACTED TO:
small trees, shrubbery, water, insects

TUFTED TITMOUSE

The decorative raccoon tail tied to the bicycle's handle bars was being attacked by a tiny, gray, mouselike bird. A female tufted titmouse intently pulled billfuls of hairs from the raccoon tail, then flitted off the porch, around the corner, and across the fence to a neighbor's yard, and then disappeared into a woodpecker hole in an apple tree.

After weaving the hair into her nest, the titmouse returned to the porch and gathered another tuft of hair from the bicycle decoration. The raccoon tail was soon bedraggled.

Meanwhile, the titmouse's mate was also on a safari, but he was searching for juicy insects from the garden. After gathering a billful, he waited until his mate disappeared again into the nesting cavity before calling her out for lunch.

Titmice have strong pair bonds, and are thought to be mated for life. During the spring and summer, they are busy raising broods of youngsters; in winter, they join a band of other titmice, chickadees, and nuthatches that forage the winter woods for insect eggs, seeds, and berries.

Among the most delightful of all garden birds to watch, the titmouse is a vivacious bundle of energy, flitting here and there, hanging upside down on tree branches in search of spider eggs, darting into the sunflower seed feeder, removing a seed, and then flipping onto a nearby branch to crack the seed open with its tiny, sharp, black bill. As soon as the shells fly, the bird is back at the feeder for another seed, or off into the woods with the rest of the gypsy band.

Tufted titmice used to be considered southern birds, but like the northern cardinal, northern mockingbird, red-bellied woodpecker, and Carolina wren, they have expanded their ranges, and are now also found throughout the Northeast and upper Midwest.

ATTRACTED TO:
tall trees, small trees, feeders, water, insects, suet, birdhouse

BLACK-CAPPED CHICKADEE

If curiosity killed the cat, then curiosity should certainly kill the chickadee. Without any doubt, the first bird to appear after hanging a new feeder, filling a pond, or planting a new flower is the black-capped chickadee. And when there is one chickadee, there is always at least another.

Yet, of all the birds in the garden, none has as pleasant a disposition, is as fearless of people, nor evokes a stronger sense of well-being than the chickadee. In other words, if there could be only one bird in the garden year-round, the chickadee would be first choice.

These winsome little gray and black 1/3-ounce balls of fluff are so quick that they can change directions in midair in 3/100th of a second. Their *chick-a-dee-dee-dee* call, and the male's spring song, *phee-bee*, are as delightful to hear as the birds are to see.

A well-shrubbed and treed yard and garden will attract a chickadee pair because they nest in the soft, rotted wood of tree cavities. They may also select a birdhouse placed at the edge of the garden, at eye level, in protective natural habitat. The 6 to 8 youngsters are as cute as any wild babies when they emerge from the nest, and to watch the parents introduce their young to sunflower seeds at bird feeders is one of the most rewarding sights of the birding year.

As autumn approaches, chickadee families band together for the winter. In the company of nuthatches and titmice, chickadees form a fellowship of roving foragers in pursuit of seeds and insect eggs. Their acrobatic, upside-down-hanging poses to get just the right angle on a spider egg provide captivating entertainment.

ATTRACTED TO:
tall trees, small trees, feeders, water, insects, suet, birdhouse

WHITE-BREASTED NUTHATCH

neat little gray bird with a black cap and white underside appears to defy gravity by walking down tree trunks head first while calling *yank, yank, yank.* This so-called "upside-down" bird seems to be searching the tree bark for insects that may have been missed by woodpeckers that hitch up the same tree trunks in the opposite direction.

Whatever the law of physics, the white-breasted nuthatch uses it to its advantage, as it is one of the common year-round residents of backyards and gardens throughout the continent. It is fond of sunflower seeds, and was named for the way it cracks them open. In contrast to the chickadees, who open seeds by holding them with its feet and hammering them with its sharp bill, and the cardinal who cracks seeds in its heavy finch bill, the nuthatch carries one seed at a time to a tree trunk where it wedges it into a crack and then hammers it open with its bill. Thus, the bird was first called "nut-hack."

During winter, white-breasted nuthatches keep close company with chickadees as bands of both roam the countryside in search of seeds and insect larvae. They typically arrive together at garden feeders where sunflower seeds and beef suet are offered.

In spring, the nuthatch pair finds a suitable cavity in a tree, 10 to 50 feet above the ground, in which they build a nest and lay as many as 10 eggs. The male's *whit-whi-whit-whi-whi* song is one of those pleasant sounds heard in nature during the vernal season.

Hatchling white-breasteds keep their parents very busy carrying insects to the nesting cavity every few minutes for about two weeks until the youngsters fledge.

ATTRACTED TO:
*tall trees, small trees,
feeders, water, insects,
suet*

HOUSE WREN

Put up ten birdhouses around the yard and garden, and by June 1, they will all be filled with sticks. This is the work of a male house wren, perhaps the most tenacious of all songbirds, the easiest to lure into the garden for the summer, and among the most delightful of feathered companions.

House wrens may be drab little brown birds, but these five-inch, 1/3-ounce flits are bundles of energy from sun up to sun down.

Male house wrens arrive from the South in suburban backyards and gardens across North America in early May, and immediately begin to sing, almost nonstop, their bubbling, chattering, repetitive burst of melody. The male will claim possession of every birdhouse in his half acre by filling each with sticks. Other possible nesting sites may include mailboxes, laundry on a clothesline, car radiators, scarecrows, boots, tin cans, watering cans, and tree cavities.

By the time a female arrives on the scene, his stubby little tail is cocked so high, and he is so full of song, that it appears that he will either blow a gasket or keel over with enthusiasm.

He takes the female on a tour of the housing possibilities, upon which he has already put down a deposit of sticks. When she chooses one, she throws out all of his sticks and builds a nest of her own. Into it she lays six or seven brown-speckled eggs, and incubates them for about 13 days.

By the time the eggs hatch, the male may have lured another female to his territory with whom he sires another nest full of youngsters.

And so it goes with house wrens in the garden. They are the very epitome of summertime, a delight to have around.

ATTRACTED TO:
*small trees, shrubbery,
insects, birdhouse*

CAROLINA WREN

It was a circuitous route the Carolina wren followed while carrying a small caterpillar in her bill—under the garage door, up to the rafters, across the ceiling, down to the tool bench, and then up to the rim of the canvas bag; a second of hesitation, and then she disappeared into the bag amidst much chittering of baby birds.

A few seconds later, the wren emerged from the bag and followed the same route in reverse to the outside, and then flew into the garden shrubbery in search of more insects. This was routine behavior for both of the Carolina wren parents that summered in a wooded central Pennsylvania backyard for many years. Between trips to the garage, the male Carolina wren sang his cheerful song, *yur tardy, yur tardy, yur tardy, yur tardy,* and *tee-dirty, tee-dirty, tee-dirty, tee-dirty.*

The name Carolina wren suggests that this largest of all eastern wrens is a resident of the Southeast, as it is. But after each mild winter, these pioneering pixies have extended their ranges north into New England and the upper Midwest. Then, following each severely cold winter, the pioneers have succumbed, and the ranges retreated back into the South.

The little birds are also adventuresome when it comes to nesting sites. Rarely more than 10 feet above the ground, the nest is a mass of leaves, twigs, and debris such as trash or even a snake skin in almost any nook or cranny the birds can negotiate. They build in mailboxes, stone walls, under bridges, and inside buildings such as garages, as well as in birdhouses, woodpecker holes and natural tree cavities. Three broods a summer are common in the South.

At garden feeders, Carolina wrens may eat bird cakes, while entertaining with their delightful, ringing song the year around.

ATTRACTED TO:
small trees, shrubbery, insects, birdhouse

CEDAR WAXWING

Sitting side by side in a garden apple tree, a pair of cedar waxwings pass a flower pedal back and forth between their bills. A few feet away, another cuddling pair pass a red berry between them. Such touching courtship these lovely birds perform.

In fact, there is nothing about cedar waxwings that is not touching … they are among the most exquisite of songbirds, not bright and flashy, but sleek and elegant. Notice the beads of red that resemble sealing wax on the tips of each wing … their waxwings.

They are among the quietest of birds, yet communicate constantly with their high pitched, chain-running calls of lisping notes strung together. They are also social birds, remaining together throughout the year in quiet flocks of 10 to 100 birds, except during their late summer breeding season. Even then, they may nest in loose colonies of a dozen or more pairs within a radius of 150 yards.

They also have an unusual system for feeding their four to five nestlings. The parent birds fill their crops with fruits and berries, and then, back at the nest, regurgitate the cargo, one item at a time, into the gaping mouths of the youngsters.

Later, when the flocks are together again to enjoy a bountiful harvest of fruits and berries, they may line up on a utility wire and pass a berry down the line from one bird to another, and then back again, until one of them gulps it down.

Instead of migrating in winter, cedar waxwings roam the countryside in search of fruits and berries, such as the orange berries of the mountain ash tree. A pond of fresh water may also bring the flock of waxwings into the garden on almost any day of the year.

ATTRACTED TO:
*tall trees, small trees,
fruit, insects, water*

RED-BELLIED WOODPECKER

*attle, rattle, rattle, rattle, rattle.* Who's making all that noise on a Sunday morning when people want to sleep?

It's just the red-bellied woodpecker sounding off on the aluminum siding, making a statement about its territory and intentions to raise a family.

Take a closer look at this living noisemaker, this jackhammer with feathers. Where's its red belly?

Well, it has been misnamed, somewhat. It has a red belly, but unless the bird is tipped up, you can't see it. A better name would have been zebra-backed woodpecker, because you can easily see that it has a zebra-striped back.

You can also see that this one is a male red-bellied because it has a red hood, while the female merely has a red nape.

Red-bellieds have been moving north in recent decades and are no longer simply birds of the Southeast. They are doing well as far north as Wisconsin and Michigan, consuming bird seeds and beef suet at garden feeders, and sipping citrus juices from orange and grapefruit halves in the spring. They may also accept an offer of birdhousing when the quarters are large enough to accommodate them.

But red-bellieds are also very good at excavating their own nesting cavities, and the European starlings know that all too well. In fact, it is common practice for a pair of starlings to watch a red-bellied pair work several days chipping out a nesting compartment in a tree trunk, and then chase the woodpeckers away, taking over the cavity for themselves.

Yet, enough red-bellieds persist and eventually raise four to five youngsters. In gardens where the parents lead their fledglings to feeders, a charming show unfolds as the youngsters learn how to feed themselves seeds and suet.

ATTRACTED TO:
tall trees, small trees, feeders, insects, suet, birdhouse

NORTHERN FLICKER

The noise was nerve shattering as the pair of northern flickers hammered a hole 30 feet up in the trunk of an old elm tree. Their rich *flicka, flicka, flicka, flicka* calls filled the air as they labored. For three days they worked very hard, until the cavity was deep enough to be a nest for the 6 to 8 youngsters they would raise.

But about the time the first egg was to be laid, a pair of European starlings took over the cavity and drove the flickers away.

This sad story of native birds being forced out of their nesting cavities by starlings is repeated over and over every year, and the victims include red-bellied woodpeckers, red-headed woodpeckers and bluebirds.

Once the flickers do establish a nest and lay eggs, it is the male that does most of the incubating, including night duty. After the eggs hatch, both parents feed the voracious youngsters a healthy diet of ants and other insects.

The northern flicker is a woodpecker, but is the least woodpeckerlike of the family. Instead of inching up tree trunks in search of food, it hops around lawns looking for ants. Its long sticky tongue helps the bird catch ants and other ground-inhabiting insects.

Otherwise, flickers are very woodpeckerlike in appearance, with long bills for pecking wood and long tails for propping themselves on trees as they excavate nesting cavities. Their most distinctive marking is a mustache that, appropriately, appears only on males. Flickers in the East have black mustaches, while flickers in the West have red mustaches. Interestingly, all baby flickers—males and females—have mustaches.

Gardeners interested in reducing their ant population might place a large birdhouse at least 10 feet above the ground, and hang a sign on it: "For rent to flickers only."

ATTRACTED TO:
tall trees, small trees, feeders, insects, suet, birdhouse

Red-headed Woodpecker

*alute!* The red, white and blue bird is passing.

If ever there was a patriotic bird . . . an all-American Uncle Sam bird, it's the red-headed woodpecker, for no other bird is all red, white and blue. Few birds are as utterly striking as they sweep across the garden.

It is well named, too. While most woodpeckers have some red on their heads, the red-headed woodpecker is the only one with an all-red head, from the shoulders up.

Yet redheads are not as common as most admirers would like. Their habitat requirements are rather strict, and they often suffer from competition with European starlings for nesting cavities. They do best in mature but open wood lots, the kind of woods that would make a great picnic site; or parkland, where huge oaks, beech and hickory grow, but with little brushy understory. It is in this kind of woodland that the redheads hammer out a nesting cavity, and if European starlings don't run them off, they will raise five youngsters that emerge from the nest with brown, not red, heads.

Red-headed woodpeckers will visit garden feeders that offer bird seed and suet, and hop around lawns in search of insects, nuts and berries. They are also known for storing or caching food, such as acorns and other nuts, in cavities to which they can return when food is less plentiful.

Unlike most other woodpeckers, red-headeds are somewhat migratory, escaping the worst of winter's cold by flying to warmer, more southerly regions in the Southeast. Their return to the North in springtime, and their distinctive *queeah, queeah, queeah* call from an old oak tree, is one of the joys of the spring season.

ATTRACTED TO:
tall trees, small trees, feeders, insects, suet

Yellow-bellied Sapsucker

Raaaaaaattttttttttttttttttttttt! Raaaaaaattttttttttttttttttttttt! A yellow-bellied sapsucker is at work. It isn't sucking sap, as its name suggests, but is drilling holes in trees to allow sap to seep out. It drills one shallow hole after another in horizontal rows. Later, the woodpeckers return to the holes to lap up the sap, along with any insects that have been attracted to the oozing tree.

But the sapsuckers are not the only ones that benefit from the so-called "sapsucker wells." Both before and after the woodpeckers return to harvest the bounty of their work, other birds and some mammals will eat the sap and insects that have collected.

Though often noisy tree drillers, yellow-bellied sapsuckers are generally quiet birds, calling a nasal *mew* as they migrate through yards and gardens between their wintering grounds in the southeast and their breeding territories in the North. But in the North, their tree drilling takes on a different purpose, as they excavate tree cavities for nesting and raising young. In selecting a nesting tree, the sapsuckers may look for trees that have been affected by tinder fungus, a disease of the heartwood of aspen and a few other trees. Such trees have a soft interior, but hard exterior, making for an ideal nesting site.

Into the gourd-shaped cavity the sapsuckers lay five to six eggs, which both parents incubate. Both parents also feed the hatchlings for about a month before they fledge.

Gardeners may take a dim view of yellow-bellied sapsuckers drilling holes in their decorative trees, but they are attractive birds to look at and interesting to watch. At garden bird feeders, they may eat beef suet and peanut butter that give them a substitute for the insects they find in the wild, and they may sip on sugar water from oriole feeders.

Attracted to:
tall trees, small trees, feeders, insects, suet

Downy Woodpecker

s one bird straddles the tree limb on one side, the other bird straddles the tree limb on the other side. Then they begin their ritualized courtship . . . the spring dance of the downy woodpeckers. To the beat of their *wick, wick, wick, wick* call, this mated pair reinforces their bonds as winter loosens its grip on the landscape.

The downy woodpecker is the smallest and best known of all American woodpeckers. Its look-alike colleague, the hairy woodpecker, is larger, with a longer, heavier bill. The male of both species sports a bright red spot at the back of his black and white head. Both are named for the feathers that surround their bills.

Downies are very energetic birds throughout the year, rattling loud, resounding whinny calls, hammering tree trunks with machine gun efficiency, and flitting hither and yon throughout open woodlands across the continent.

At garden feeders, downies may be very tame, sometimes clinging to feeders while taking hulled sunflower seeds from the tubes as human admirers watch from only a few inches away.

Though the downies begin their courtship displays early in spring, even while the snow is still piled deep in the woodlands, they do not get to serious nesting chores until later. Both excavate the nesting cavity with their short but sharp black bills, and both incubate the four to five pure white eggs laid on a few chips of wood. Fledgling downies look larger and tidier than their worn-out parents when they are introduced to seeds and beef suet at backyard feeders.

Unlike many garden birds, downies remain in residence throughout the four seasons, gleaning insects that they find on tree bark while shinnying up and down the trunks. They also tend to be frequent visitors to garden feeders where they relish beef suet and bird seed.

ATTRACTED TO:
tall trees, small trees, feeders, insects, suet

SCRUB JAY

The scrub jay flew to the picnic table, picked up an earring, and flew away with it in its bill. "Hey, come back with my earring!" cried the camper. But it was too late. The scrub jay was well away from the campground, probably secreting the earring in a cache containing other interesting, if not valuable, stolen objects.

This behavior for the crestless blue jay of Florida and the Southwest is typical of most jays, all of which are members of the crow family. Campers, picnickers, hikers, and gardeners have to be careful about leaving bright and shiny objects lying in sight of these avian camp robbers. Not only are they intelligent birds, but their long, strong bills are adept at picking up such objects, and stashing them out of sight.

The Florida scrub jay is a subspecies of the western scrub jay, and is endangered because its Florida scrub habitat has been shrunk by development. Because of this, the Florida jays have been forced to adapt to crowded conditions, much like apartment dwellers in New York City. Youngsters will remain with their parents for one or more years, until a territory of about 25 acres opens up for them. Until then, they remain at home, helping their parents defend the family territory and raise the next brood.

In the West, where scrub jays are common and where there is an abundance of habitat, the youngsters leave their parents' territories as soon as they are old enough to take care of themselves.

In both Florida and the Southwest, scrub jays visit gardens where they can enjoy sunflower seeds, suet and a drink or bath in bird pools. Their loud and raspy *sheek, sheek, sheek* call is better known than the male's soft, sweet, high-pitched whisper song to his mate.

ATTRACTED TO:
small trees, shrubbery, feeders, water, insects, suet

BLUE JAY

lert! Alert! Here comes a blue jay … all other birds, fly! Escape! The bully bird is coming.

Its *jay, jay, jay* call is a loud, brash, and demanding pronouncement. Henry David Thoreau, perhaps somewhat unjustly, described the call as an "unrelenting steel-cold scream of a jay, unmelted, that never flows into a song. A sort of wintry trumpet, screaming cold, hard, tense, frozen music, like the winter sky itself."

If there is such a thing as a bully bird, the blue jay is it. Yet, this cunning, mischievous, thieving, cruel, boastful, quarreling, treacherous, wanton behavior is much like that of other members of the crow family, to which it belongs. And like other crows … ravens, magpies, nutcrackers and rooks … blue jays are very intelligent.

Take their communications system. The amazing repertoire of a blue jay, in addition to its screaming *jay* call, includes a far more musical and quieter bell-like *tull-ull*, which it utters while raising and lowering its head. Females give a rapid clicking call that sounds like *tea-cup*. Then there is the whisper call, a musical vocalization a male gives when courting a female.

Surprisingly, blue jays are generally very quiet while nesting and raising young. So quiet, in fact, that they are rarely seen or heard during spring and early summer.

Though 75 percent of what they eat is vegetable matter . . . nuts, fruit, berries and grains . . . blue jays will also eat insects, snails, fish, frogs, mice, and the eggs and tiny nestlings of other birds.

Despite its bad reputation, the blue jay is one of the most beautiful birds in North America. Its brilliant azure blue body seems to be a statement of confidence and strength. Here is a royal bird that adds a great deal of interest and excitement to any garden.

ATTRACTED TO:
tall trees, small trees, shrubbery, feeders, water, suet, insects

MOURNING DOVE

The teenage mourning dove was just out of the nest, loafing on the feeder tray, wondering if being grown up was all that it was cracked up to be. No longer did he have pigeon milk pumped into his throat every few minutes by his parents. Now he was on his own, and now he had to gather the seeds for himself, and all of that seemed too much of a bother. So he loafed, which mourning doves do a great deal.

The classic dove of North America, and a close relative to the extinct passenger pigeon, the silky, buffy-gray mourning doves are everywhere, and it seems no garden is without them. Named for the slow, mournful *cwoo-ah, cwoo, cwoo, cwoo* calls of the males, mourning dove populations are counted by the calls of individual males in what is known as a "coo count."

Where there is a *cwoo*, there is a pair of doves, often courting in a most demonstrative display. The male, slightly larger than the female, puffs up all his feathers, flashes his iridescent neck, and towers over the female while following her around the garden. She, meanwhile, pretends not to notice, and goes about feeding or gathering nesting material.

Together they build a flimsy stick nest on an evergreen bough, and raise two youngsters in each of several broods a year.

In 30 states, mourning doves are classified as game birds and are hunted each autumn. Surprisingly, populations of doves in those states remain as stable as populations in states where they are protected as songbirds.

Bird seeds of any kind interest mourning doves, and given a platform feeder on which they can perch, the birds will remain in gardens throughout the year, content to eat, drink, bathe in garden ponds, and otherwise loaf the days away.

ATTRACTED TO:
tall trees, small trees, shrubbery, ground cover, feeders, water

NORTHERN BOBWHITE

The good fortune of having bobwhite quail in your garden doesn't increase your property taxes, but it surely enhances your quality of life.

No other North American game bird has endeared itself more than the classic quail of the South. No southern plantation is worthy of the title unless it has bobwhites the year around.

For most of the year, these plump little chickenlike birds live in small flocks, or coveys, of a dozen or more birds. At night, they form a protective circle, tails pointed in, heads out. Should danger threaten, the covey flushes, with each bird flying in the direction it is pointed, scattering the flock in all directions. To reassemble the covey, the members whistle a slurred, two-part gathering call.

In spring, the clarion *bob, bob-white* whistle engulfs the landscape, as the covey breaks up into pairs and scatters into nesting territories. The most fortunate of gardeners have their own bobwhites, and watch as the seemingly devoted pair build a nest in a hollow on the ground, lining it with grasses that arch above for better concealment. Some 14 to 16 creamy white eggs are incubated by both parents for 23 to 24 days before all hatch together. As soon as the chicks dry, the tiny balls of brown fluff follow their parents away from the nest, never to return. The families join other families to form coveys in the fall.

Bobwhites eat grains, weed seeds and small insects from the wild, but will come to ground feeders in backyards for cracked corn and other bird seeds. They will also be attracted to gardens where water is available for drinking and bathing.

ATTRACTED TO:
small trees, shrubbery, ground cover, feeders, water

RING-NECKED PHEASANT

trutting as if he owned the place, a gaudy-colored male ring-necked pheasant sauntered into the garden, looked around, and then began to eat the waste seeds on the ground beneath the feeders. It was a very cold day in January, but the sun was bright, and the reflections off the bird's array of colorful feathers was breathtaking.

No shy newcomer, the confident cock was king of the feeders whenever he was there. Songbirds and gray squirrels alike gave him a wide berth, or suffered the consequences of being ruefully run off.

The king in his regal robes visited the garden every day for several weeks, and then, as the weather moderated, he made less frequent visits and then not at all. Was he off attending to a court of dull mottled brown hens?

As spring approached, the courting male's crow, which sounds like a rooster's and is followed by a whir of his wings, was heard from the nearby cornfield. The hens in his harem would produce 10 to 12 chicks each that would be ready to leave the nests as soon as they hatched. In seven more days, they would fly. By summer's end, the cultivated fields would be well populated with teenage pheasants running up and down the rows of crops.

During the nesting season, ring-necked pheasants eat a great many insects and green plants; the rest of the year, they fatten up on waste grain, berries and weed seeds.

Though ring-necked pheasants are not natives, having been first introduced in Oregon from China in 1881, they have become the number one game bird in North America. Their inclination to run rather than fly, and then when flushed explode into the sky, make them a worthy challenge for any sportsman and his dog.

ATTRACTED TO:
fields, shrubbery, ground cover, feeders, insects

KILLDEER

Fido scampers across the lawn, past the garden, and out the driveway for his morning constitutional. Suddenly the dog pulls up sharply, and freezes in a perfect point at something at the edge of the driveway.

That something is a female killdeer that seems to be injured, her wings and tail spread wide, she calls a pathetic *trrrrrrrrrr*. Floundering around on the ground, the killdeer limps away from the dog. Fido follows. The killdeer keeps moving just ahead of the curious canine.

The killdeer is performing a broken-wing-act, a defense behavior for which this bird is well known. With wings drooped and body limp, the killdeer lures the unsuspecting dog away from four hatchlings that are crouched and motionless in the gravel of the driveway. Fido pursues. When the bird is a safe distance away from the chicks, she recovers and flies away from the dog, calling *kill-dee, kill-dee, kill-dee*, the call for which the bird is named.

The killdeer is a shorebird. Yet it most often lives some distance from water, and close to people. Its natural habitat includes gardens, lawns, golf courses, parking lots and cultivated fields. On farms, it spends a great deal of time following tractors around fields where grubs and other insects are turned up by the machinery.

When the look-alike killdeer pair is ready to nest, they select a gravel area where the stones look most like the four eggs they will lay. Because a nest would only draw attention to the eggs, no nest is built. When the young hatch and dry off, they are ready to run, and leave the nest forever. For the next month or so, the offspring, each resembling a little ball of cotton on two toothpicks, follow their parents around the garden in search of insects to eat.

ATTRACTED TO:
open fields, insects

CANADA GOOSE

he injured female Canada goose landed on the lake, but could not take off. She was grounded, but not alone. Her mate remained with her most of the time. On the rare occasions that he did leave her, he would always return to the lake by nightfall. The pair had sufficient food, as they grazed the grassy lawns, and tipped up for aquatic salads in the water.

As winter approached, other geese joined the pair on the lake for days at a time, but then moved on, leaving the pair behind. Eventually, the lake began to freeze, and the pair was forced into a smaller and smaller pool of open water.

Finally, one morning in November, the lake was locked up tight with ice, and the geese were gone. What ultimately happened to them is not known. What is known is that the pair demonstrated the strong pair bonds typical of Canada geese.

Traditionally, Canada geese migrate north in the spring into the Canadian Arctic, where they nest and raise five to six young. Then, as soon as the young can fly, the goose family joins other families, and returns to the United States for the winter.

Recently, Canada goose numbers have grown significantly across the continent, and some populations have become non-migratory, remaining in the same general area of the United States throughout the year. Those geese have caused problems when they have fouled golf courses, lakes and reservoirs, and grazed on green garden plants. For the most part, however, Canada geese that visit lawns and gardens are a thing of beauty, and unless they are threatening plants, their presence should be a rewarding experience for homeowners and gardeners.

ATTRACTED TO:
wetlands, open fields

MALLARD

eneath a low-growing yew branch, a hen mallard and her hatchling brood of 10 ducklings lend exciting new life to a suburban back-yard garden. The family has been in residence since the brown-streaked hen, accompanied by her handsome green-headed mate, waddled into the garden, selected the nesting site, and began lining the spot with grasses nearly a month earlier.

When the ducklings dry shortly after hatching, they will follow their mother out of the nest to the nearest water, and grow up as the summer unfolds.

Meanwhile, the drake will join other males in a bachelor flock, and change his breeding plumage for a new garb that will take him into winter.

The most common and widespread of all North American ducks, mallards are increasingly seeking suburban garden habitat as nesting and rearing sites, under shrubbery, in window wells, and in wild corners of yards. Gardeners are the benefactors, as the green-headed drake and his subdued but resourceful mate increase the beauty and wildlife excitement of any backyard.

They also enhance the natural sounds, as a variety of calls are emitted from the ducks. The drake speaks a *yeeb* along with a low *kwek*; while both sound the classic *quack, quack, quack* when startled.

When feeding on water, mallards typically tip up to glean aquatic vegetation from beneath the surface, thus the term "puddle ducks." On land, they often nibble tender green shoots in agricultural fields, and later they eat waste grain left from the harvest. Mallards are particularly fond of dried kernels of field corn. So much so, that some admiring people make a regular ritual of "feeding the ducks" by carrying pails of corn to spots where mallards congregate, and feeding the fearless beggars from their hands.

ATTRACTED TO:
wetlands, open fields

WOOD DUCK

After sitting in the entrance of the duck house for half an hour, checking on potential danger in the area, the female wood duck drops to the ground 30 feet below, and calls.

Instantly, little fuzzy balls of yellow down appear at the bird house entrance, leap into midair flapping their stubby wings as they fall to the ground, and then bounce like tennis balls before coming to rest beside the hen.

When all 16 or so ducklings are out, the mother wood duck utters another command, and all the babies follow her into the water and to the cover of the marsh beyond.

When a female duckling jumps out of the nesting cavity or duck house in which she was hatched, she is imprinted on that site. The following spring, after spending the winter hundreds of miles to the south, she will lead her mate back to the exact nesting location where she was hatched. If that nest is occupied by her mother or a sibling, she will find another site nearby in which to lay eggs.

After a month of incubation by the hen, all the eggs hatch on the same day, and the ducklings, like their mother before them, will jump out of the nest and follow her to the water where they will grow up. In fall, they'll migrate south for the winter, and then return the following spring to start the cycle over again.

Wood ducks are tree ducks, and can be a fascinating part of any garden tableau, as when the drake accompanies the hen to the duck house or tree cavity each morning and evening during the nesting period. The bonanza, however, is seeing the downy ducklings leap from the house and scurry after their mother in a cascade of fluffy yellow and brown down.

ATTRACTED TO:
wetlands, tall trees, birdhouse

AMERICAN KESTREL

Quietly perched on a telephone wire, the small falcon eyes the garden vegetation below. Suddenly it leaps off the wire, folds its long, pointed wings, drops toward the ground like a rock, pulls up at a height of 10 feet, hovers for a second, then dives to the ground.

With its wings still spread on the ground, the American kestrel clutches a large grasshopper in its talons. The exquisitely marked male looks around, flaps its wings, and is airborne again, returning to the wire where it daintily eats its prey.

Our best known and most often seen raptor, the American kestrel is a regular visitor to many gardens across North America. This smallest falcon, no larger than a robin, was once known as "sparrow hawk," because its varied diet includes the occasional sparrow or other songbird. But kestrels are considered beneficial to gardeners for the number of insects, mice, and reptiles they consume. Their *killy, killy, killy* calls add interesting natural sounds to the garden environment.

Both the reddish male with his blue wing coverts, and the overall reddish female have double black stripes on their faces. They are the only falcons that nest in tree cavities, woodpecker holes, or birdhouses. Inside, they use little or no nesting material upon which the female lays four to five eggs.

Parent kestrels are very attentive, one keeping guard from a nearby tree perch, while the other carries food in its talons to the cavity full of hungry nestlings. Fledgling kestrels are among the most appealing of all baby birds, marked like their parents with blue and reddish feathers and facial stripes.

Gardeners interested in kestrels may attract them by hanging a large birdhouse on a pole at the edge of an open field or garden, 20 to 30 feet above the ground.

ATTRACTED TO:
open fields, birdhouse

SCREECH OWL

very winter evening, like clockwork, a screech owl appears in the entrance to the wood duck house, the setting sun casting a reddish glow over its plumage. Its sleepy yellow eyes are deceptive as the diminutive owl makes mental notes on every movement around it, particularly those of the songbirds that come and go to the feeders. If a careless mouse scurries across the snow below it, the ball of downy feathers will leave the house early, perhaps returning immediately with dinner. Otherwise, it remains sitting in the entrance, patiently waiting for darkness.

Every March 15, also like clockwork, the same wood duck house is cleaned out in preparation for the return of nesting wood ducks. More often than not, the musty wood chips inside contain a variety of feathers—a few red, as in cardinal; a few blue, as in blue jay; and a few black and white, as in downy woodpecker. Screechy eats well.

One year, the remains of a robin were found, the first recorded robin of that spring. Another year, Screechy himself, or herself, was in the house, sitting on a clutch of five eggs. There would be no wood ducks in the house that year. But that was okay, because screech owls are really more interesting to watch as they feed their young than are the wood ducks that are seen only when coming and going at dawn and dusk during incubation. And the baby screech owls are as endearing as any ducklings on the day they leave the house and sit around in the trees waiting to be fed.

Screech owls do not screech. They sing a tremulous whinny song that can be heard in the cold night air starting in late December.

Though screech owls' eating habits may be less than pleasing to some whose goal is to attract garden songbirds, their presence does add a delightful and dynamic dimension to any garden scene.

ATTRACTED TO:
tall trees, small trees, birdhouse

National Wildlife Federation Backyard Wildlife Habitat Program

For more than 20 years, the National Wildlife Federation has been a leader in helping people develop wildlife habitats in their backyards. Through feature stories in *National Wildlife* magazine and direct educational efforts, the National Wildlife Federation has fostered efforts to plant wildlife habitat, install water areas, and provide food for wildlife in backyards throughout the country.

Thousands of backyards have been certified by the National Wildlife Federation when additional cover, food or water have been provided to benefit wildlife. It is not necessary to achieve a full-grown habitat before seeking certification; even initial efforts are of value to wildlife and worthy of recognition in the Backyard Wildlife Habitat Program.

If you would like to register your bird garden as an official Backyard Wildlife Habitat, and receive a handsome, personalized certificate with your own habitat number, simply fill out the accompanying application and send it to:

National Wildlife Federation
Backyard Wildlife Habitat Program
1400 16th Street, N.W.
Washington, DC 20036-2266

BACKYARD WILDLIFE HABITAT PROGRAM
APPLICATION • FOR • CERTIFICATION

NAME _____   HABITAT # _____

ADDRESS _____

CITY _____ COUNTY _____

STATE/PROVINCE _____ ZIP/POSTAL CODE _____

TELEPHONE _____

PROPERTY SIZE (Sq. Ft. or Acres) _____

OFFICE USE:
fee rcvd. —
certified —
c.s. —
key words —

HAVE YOU EVER APPLIED FOR CERTIFICATION BEFORE ___ YES ___ NO IF YES LIST STATE OR HABITAT NO. _____

Take heart, you needn't be a zoologist or botanist to fill out this application. We're anxious to reward your efforts in providing habitat for wildlife where you live or work as soon as we can. Do the best you can to fill out the application—if there are problems with it (and there rarely are) we'll get back to you with some suggestions. Within 4-6 weeks of receiving your application we'll forward to you a beautiful personalized certificate suitable for framing.

1. FOOD/*Plantings and Feeders*

A. Do your best to list those plants on your property which might provide wildlife foods such as acorns, berries, nuts, seeds, buds or nectar.

LARGE TREES	NO.	SMALL TREES	NO.	SHRUBS	NO.	ANNUALS & PERENNIALS	NO.

B. List the type and number of feeders and foods that you provide for wildlife.

FEEDER TYPE	NO.	FOODS		VISITED BY

2. WATER/*Drinking, Bathing*

A. We provide water: ☐ Year Round   ☐ Seasonally

B. We provide water   ☐ Bird Bath   ☐ Water dripping into a bird bath
in the following ways: ☐ Spring   ☐ Wildlife Pool   ☐ Pond   ☐ Stream
☐ Other _____

Working for the Nature of Tomorrow®
NATIONAL WILDLIFE FEDERATION 1400 Sixteenth Street, N.W., Washington, D.C. 20036-2266

3. COVER/*Places to Hide*

A. We provide wind and weather breaks and places for wildlife to hide from predators in the following manner.

☐ Dense Shrubs (which types?) _____

☐ Evergreens (which types?) _____

☐ Brush Piles   ☐ Log Piles   ☐ Rock Piles/Walls   ☐ Ground Covers

☐ Meadow, Scrub or Prairie Patch   ☐ Other (Describe) _____

4. PLACES TO RAISE YOUNG

A. We provide the following for nesting birds, denning mammals, egg-laying reptiles and amphibians, fish, butterflies, and other insects and invertebrates.

☐ Mature Trees (which types?) _____

☐ Small Trees (which types?) _____

☐ Shrub Masses (which types?) _____

☐ Trees with   ☐ Dens in Ground/Rock   ☐ Wildlife Pool/Pond   ☐ Meadow, Prairie or
     Nest/Den Cavities   Scrub Patch

                                                                                   Size _____ sq. ft.

☐ Nesting Boxes   ☐ Nesting Shelves.
     Which animals use them? (birds, squirrels, bats, frogs, dragonflies, etc.) _____

☐ Plants for butterfly caterpillars (which types?) _____

Please include a rough sketch or landscape diagram of your yard. If you would like, enclose some snap shots of your habitat and of you, your family or friends working in and enjoying your habitat. We cannot return the photos or sketch however, so please be sure you have duplicates for your own use.

Remember to submit the $15 Program Enrollment Fee (check or money order) to cover our processing and handling costs. Make check payable & send to: National Wildlife Federation, 1400 16th Street, N.W., Washington, DC 20036-2266.

Beyond Your Certification....

The health of our environment depends on how we treat it. To get the most from your wildlife attracting efforts while practicing an environmental "good neighbor" policy in your community, try to put the landscape suggestions below into practice.

- Eliminate most turf grasses.
- Conserve water.
- Rely on natural pest control.

- Use less commercial fertilizer.
- Recycle your leaves, prunings, grass clippings, and if possible, kitchen scraps, into compost and mulches.
- Grow native plants.

For tips on how to nurture an environmentally sensible landscape, refer to NWF's Backyard Wildlife Habitat Information Packet.

Backyard Wildlife Habitats can be anywnere in your yard—front, back or all of it. If you don't have property or want to work on another habitat project, consider adopting a school, a business, a zoo, botanical garden, homeowner's common ground, natural area or nursing home. If you're involved with a habitat project in a non-traditional setting, let us hear about it. If you'd like information about a school or other community habitats, write us for an idea sheet.